GOLD MEDAL KILLER

Diana Franklin
10/14/11

James Howard Snook. Reprinted, with permission, from *The Columbus Dispatch* Archives.

GOLD MEDAL KILLER

The Shocking True Story of the Ohio State Professor –
an Olympic Champion – and His Coed Lover

DIANA BRITT FRANKLIN
WITH NANCY PENNELL

MARQUETTE BOOKS LLC
Spokane, Washington

Copyright © 2010 Diana Britt Franklin

All rights reserved. No part of this publication may be reproduced, stored in a retrieval system, or transmitted in any form or by any means, electronic, mechanical, photocopying, microfilming, recording, or otherwise, without permission of the author.

Printed in the United States of America

Library of Congress Control Number 2010924012

ISBN: 978-0-9826597-2-4

Cover photo illustration by Ted Kibble
Back cover photographs by Mary Circelli
Interior design by Marquette Books

Published by
Marquette Books
3107 East 62nd Avenue
Spokane, Washington 99223
509-443-7057 (voice) • 509-448-2191 (fax)
books@marquettebooks.org • www.MarquetteBooks.org

To our children

CONTENTS

ACKNOWLEDGMENTS ix
FOREWORD by Judge Teresa L. Liston, ret. xi
1. The Shooter 1
2. 'We Just Seen It!' 8
3. Theora 16
4. The Accused 21
5. 'Read All About It!' 34
6. A 'Scholastic Shylock' 41
7. A Very Difficult Problem 48
8. Getting a Jury 57
9. The Direct Cause of Death 67
10. Journalists Take the Stand 78
11. The Stoolie 84
12. Mother and Wife 90
13. In His Defense – Part One 94
14. In His Defense – Part Two 101
15. Letters from Mabel 111
16. In the Coupe 120
17. The Slap 131
18. 'Never Burn' 136
19. Done in a Dozen Minutes 148
20. Nary a Thought 152
21. At Peace with God 160
22. A Logical Conclusion 169
   EPILOGUE 175
   AFTERWORD – THURBER'S TALE 181
   BIBLIOGRAPHY 184
   INDEX 186
   ABOUT THE AUTHORS 191

✱ ACKNOWLEDGMENTS

More than two dozen newspaper reporters who covered the Snook case deserve our recognition. The list of journalists appears in the Bibliography.

Numerous librarians deserving of special recognition include those at the Cleveland Public Library; Special Collections, Cleveland State University Library, Linda Deitch and the editorial library of *The Columbus Dispatch,* and the many great librarians at the Columbus (Ohio) Metropolitan Library; Ohio Historical Society, Columbus; Upper Arlington (Ohio) Library, The Ohio State University Archives and the New York Public Library.

Others to whom we are indebted for making this a better book include John J. "Jack" Chester, Luke Feck, Mary Anne Edwards, Phil Rudell, Richard Carson, Piri Halasz, Trisha Brown, Sandy Clary, Cheryl Pentella and Charles C. Howard.

✱ | FOREWORD

In the heat of July and August 1929, Columbus, Ohio was the unlikely setting for "one of the most sordid murder trials ever staged in an American courtroom." An Olympic champion and full professor at The Ohio State University stood accused of bludgeoning to death his co-ed lover of three years. This was the stuff of movies and novels, and the public could not get enough of it. Hundreds stood in lines for hours, hoping to get a courtroom seat to watch a young, politically ambitious and popular prosecutor wage battle with a "dream team" of experienced and eloquent defense attorneys.

Such intense public fascination with the spectacle of a murder trial is not solely a contemporary "post-O.J." phenomenon. From Elizabethan England, where people traveled to hear proceedings at the Old Bailey as a form of entertainment, to the current legal commentary of television pundits and televised trials, people have been attracted to unique human drama. Thus, it comes as no surprise to me, a trial court judge of many years, to often witness people's continued absorption with trials.

I can imagine no greater attention to a trial, however, than that paid to the shocking charges accusing Dr. James Snook of the murder of Theora Hix. *Gold Medal Killer*, with both factual and legal accuracy, recounts this compelling story of lust, drugs, murder, and the law. Taken from the transcripts of the proceeding, as well as the detailed journalistic coverage of the case, this gripping book takes the reader from the time of the discovery of an unknown dead woman to the execution of the defendant in the Ohio Penitentiary's electric chair.

The State sought not only the conviction, but also the execution, of a respected member of the Columbus and Ohio State University communities, alleging that a calculated and pre-meditated murder had taken place. The defense argued that the defendant was not guilty by reason of temporary insanity or, if guilty, had lacked the malice and premeditation needed to justify the death penalty under then existing Ohio law.

The murder trial of Dr. James Snook took place in a time when mere mention of matters sexual was deemed too lurid to print in respectable newspapers. The more than 30 journalists who wrote daily about the trial knew that much of the defendant's salacious testimony about his relationship with Miss Hix and his account of the specific details surrounding her death would never get into print. Instead, they found themselves detailing the fashions of the ladies in attendance as carefully as the legal arguments asserted by the prosecution and defense.

This also was a time when the respect for the legal system was significantly different from today. Editorials frequently appeared throughout the trial commending the judge for his abilities in presiding over the case. No criticisms of the judge or jury were the subject of daily accounts by "legal commentators".

Gold Medal Killer reminds us, however, of a time in legal history when society valued speedy justice above all. Compared to the careful and deliberate legal proceedings held today before an execution takes place, this trial resulted in the execution of a man a mere 260 days after the alleged crime took place and after only 12 minutes of life-or-death deliberation by the jury.

Since Miranda rights to protect the accused had yet to be mandated – the United States Supreme Court did so in 1966 – this was a time when the prosecuting attorney could coerce a confession after a 22-hour interrogation, deny the accused the presence of his attorneys during questioning, and in frustration strike him in the face when he refused to confess. Such actions today would be unheard of. They would be the subject of strenuous defense objections and would prohibit the introduction of any "confession" of the accused at trial. However, the prosecutor was able to have the jury hear of this confession and simply stated that he had "offered his apology to the defendant, and it was accepted by him."

Relatives of both the prosecutor and his chief investigator were members of the Franklin County Grand Jury that issued the indictment against Dr. Snook. This violation of our firmly held principals demanding an independent and impartial review by a Grand Jury would certainly raise objections today. However, during the trial of Dr. Snook, they were not even the subject of legal arguments or appeal.

Finally, it was a time when no forensic analysis of the evidence was available to either the prosecution or defense. This left the exact cause of death an unanswered question. It further, and more importantly, resulted in the central legal issue of the defendant's "premeditation" unable to be determined within any degree of scientific certainty.

Was Dr. Snook guilty of the murder of Theora Hix? Of this I have no doubt. It is the circumstances of her death, however, and the conflicting accounts of the actions and intentions of this puzzling man that lie at the center of the most important question raised by this case and by *Gold Medal Killer:* Should Dr. Snook have died in Ohio's electric chair? You be the judge.

Judge Teresa L. Liston, ret.
Franklin County (Ohio) Municipal Court
February, 2010

1 | THE SHOOTER

In slippered feet, James Snook stepped out onto his porch, took a short breath of the June morning air and looked to the top of the trees surrounding his sturdy brick double at 349 W. 10th Ave. in Columbus. A light breeze, he observed. Good. It was a fine day for a shooting match.

He reached down and picked up *The Ohio State Journal*: "Class of '29 to Pass Into History Today" was the front-page headline that caught his eye. He was glad he was not required to attend Ohio State University's commencement exercises, although many other members of the faculty elected to do so.

As she prepared breakfast in the kitchen, his wife casually asked about his schedule. Helen knew her husband would be competing in yet another pistol-shooting match, but which one she did not know – nor cared, really. She was used to his absences: for pistol shooting, for his work as a professor at Ohio State University's College of Veterinary Medicine, for the writing and editing of articles for monthly outdoors magazines and for other self-satisfying interests.

"It's another team competition sponsored by *The Citizen*," he informed her casually. The Columbus afternoon newspaper was underwriting a shooting match between the Columbus Police Division and a civilian team, led by Snook and his friend, Ray Bracken. Both were world record-holders with the handgun.

"So, you will be home for dinner?"

"I'm not sure."

Missing dinner at home with his wife of seven years had become a rather common occurrence. She had thought – and hoped – that after the birth of their daughter, Mary "Jill," now 23 months old, he would stay closer to home, but such was not the case.[1] In fact, Helen saw even less of him. She sensed that he was pulling away at a time when parenthood should intensify the vows they made to each other.

Helen Thatcher Marple of nearby Newark, Ohio, had been a sixth-grade teacher before she married Snook on September 11, 1922, at the King Avenue Methodist Church in Columbus. Those who knew her best saw a woman of genteel background, sweet and uncomplicated. She was intelligent, dedicated and a graduate of Ohio State University with a degree in education. She wore clothes tailored to her pleasingly plump frame and often wore a fashionable brimmed cloche that framed her fair countenance. Some might describe her style as homely, but she displayed a breed of kindness that induced harmony, and she carried herself with dignity, chin high, even in unhappy times.

Many believed James and Helen to be a good match. He was meticulous. He liked order and consistency. His clothes, he insisted, were to be kept impeccably clean and neat, and she willingly met his demands, being fastidious herself. She saw to it that the tidy, parsimonious professor always had a clean, starched collar, even when he was going to be on the shooting range. In competition he most often wore a three-piece suit and a flat cap or fedora, as did many of the other shooters of the day.

Snook's thoughts returned to the pistol match a few hours hence. Ray Bracken, a local lumberman, was an outstanding marksman, and for more than a dozen years, he and Snook, both members of the Columbus

---

[1] A son, born earlier, died in infancy.

Revolver Club, had fired tens of thousands of rounds together, both in practice and in competition. In fact, they were teammates on the victorious 1920 United States Olympic pistol-shooting team when the competition was held in Beverloo, Belgium, outside of Antwerp.

The Antwerp Olympics, the first after World War I, were noteworthy for several reasons. The Olympic flag with five interlocking rings was used for the first time; a competitor took the Olympic oath for the first time; and the release of white doves, signifying peace, became an official part of the opening ceremonies.

Bracken made USA's five-member pistol-shooting team in the July qualifying matches at Quantico, Virginia; Snook was selected as an alternate. When one of the chosen was unable to toe the line in Olympic competition, Snook took his mark.

He excelled. In the team competition for the military pistol at 30 meters, the USA beat Greece and Switzerland. In the team match for free pistol firing at 50 meters, the team again took the gold, this time over Sweden and Brazil.

Winning two Olympic gold medals was quite an achievement for the 40-year-old native son of South Lebanon, Ohio, a rural community about 30 miles northeast of Cincinnati. Snook was born there September 17, 1879,[2] the only son of Albert L. and Mary Keever Snook. Six years later the couple had a daughter, Bertha, who married Arthur Hamilton. In the early 1930s, he served as speaker of the Ohio House of Representatives. The Snook family tree also includes a distant relationship to John D. Rockefeller, founder of Standard Oil.

"Jimmy," as the locals knew him, was polite, studious and quiet as a teen. "He was the most easygoing boy at the school [South Lebanon High School] who never got into any trouble," said the grocer, who had Jimmy carry groceries from the village store in the center of town, down tree-lined streets to the homes of neighbors. "He always minded his folks."

---

[2] As an adult, Snook lied about his age on occasion, including on his marriage license, preferring to be somewhat younger. This birth date is correct, however.

In school Jimmy was a loner of sorts, not paying much attention to classmates of either gender. He often failed to keep a date with a girl, and rather than hang out with the boys, he preferred to jump on a mare and ride off by himself to practice shooting. More than once, neighbors complained that the boy's target practice – sometimes from horseback – endangered their cattle. As often as not, though, he would ride to the nearby King Powder Co., which produced gunpowder for the Peters Cartridge Co., and practice target shooting there.

Sanford J. Brown, a ruddy-faced high-school teacher, admitted to boxing Jimmy's ears on occasion when he failed to prepare his Latin homework. "When he came to me for his pre-college credits, I hesitated to give them to him," Brown recalled. "But I decided to stretch the blanket, and I'm glad I did. Later I was proud of him."

Albert Snook owned some 220 acres of prime farmland and a small corn-canning factory. You might say – and townspeople did – that he was "well-to-do." His family had been entrenched in Warren County since 1781, having traveled overland by wagon from Monmouth County, New Jersey. Members of the Snook clan served in the Civil War as well as in the War of 1812. The family's hilltop home was comfortable and spacious, with a large wraparound porch. Around its foundation and down the walk were plantings of gay petunias, nasturtiums and zinnias. It was "the finest home in town," some townspeople said. Others thought the Snook family "uppity."

A racetrack on the farm gave evidence to Albert Snook's lifelong interest in racehorses. The track attracted people from nearby communities, and visitors to the Snook home often spoke of nothing but horses. Jimmy loved being a part of it. The talk and the animals sparked his interest in veterinary medicine, and it was to become his lifelong occupation.

Before settling down in that field, however, he earned a two-year commercial business degree at Nelson's Business College in Cincinnati, returned to the farm for three years and then entered Ohio State University in 1905 at the urging of a neighbor, a veterinarian. Snook earned his doctorate in veterinary medicine three years later. The 1908 university yearbook, *Makio*, noted that the tight-lipped and already thin-haired graduate was a member of the Veterinary Medical Society, Sigma Phi Epsilon and Alpha Psi, the veterinary fraternity he helped found. It also noted:

> *His friends, they are many.*
> *His foes – are there any?*

In the spring of 1908, Governor Andrew L. Harris called out Cavalry Troop B of the Ohio National Guard, to which Snook belonged, to quell violence along the Ohio River. Marauding bands of "night riders," intent on destroying tobacco fields and warehouses linked to the American Tobacco Co. monopoly, terrorized residents along Ohio's southern border. The arrival from Columbus of Troop B – self-described as "men who are red-blooded and real go-getters" – soon quashed the disturbances.

With a view to earning a teaching position at Ohio State, Snook entered Cornell University in Ithaca, New York, in the fall of 1908, but after a year returned to the farm yet again. On January 1, 1910, he secured a position as a teaching assistant in the College of Veterinary Medicine at Ohio State and gradually moved up the ladder to assistant professor and then full professor in 1921.

While at the college, he invented a surgical instrument for the spaying of female cats and dogs. It became known as the Snook hook, and it is still used by veterinarians for performing ovariohysterectomies.

As a student at Ohio State, he became interested in handguns, and it wasn't long before he became a champion at pistol shooting. By 1911 Snook had established a world's record with the revolver. A year later, he won five matches with "remarkable scores" at the national championships, competed successfully in international matches and clearly established himself as one of the nation's premier shooters.

"Through all of this shooting he has made careful studies and readily admits that his success in winning so many big matches is not all due to simply holding steady and pulling the trigger," observed *Hunter-Trader-Trapper*.

In the spring of 1917, the lanky marksman became gun and ammunition editor of that popular monthly magazine, receiving $100 a month. In announcing his appointment, the magazine noted that as a teenager Snook was "extremely accurate" with a shotgun and victorious "against high-class shooters" in Ohio competitions. The magazine overlooked what Snook himself claimed as his first love, namely fly-fishing, at which he also excelled.

Because of his association with the university, Snook often chose to use a pen name on the many articles he wrote. The name varied from time to time, but it always included the word *king*, such as *Kingfisher, Kingman,* and *Wesley King.*

As an undergraduate at Ohio State, he became associated with the Military Aeronautics School on campus, where he taught rifle and small-arms shooting to Army recruits during World War I. He refused an Army commission in order to remain at the university during the war.

The magazine continued: "With the Scheutzen target rifle[3] he captured the Peters Challenge Trophy several times. This beautiful cup represents the Indoor Rifle Championship of Ohio and Indiana. At present [it] adorns the doctor's desk where it seems to rest quite securely."

Also on his desk at Ohio State lay a small pistol made of spouting tin. Students and associates alike witnessed Snook's accuracy with the toy, shooting rubber bands at houseflies. On occasion he also took a real pistol from his desk and shot birds out of trees surrounding the veterinary school, just for amusement.

Edward J. Yantis of the Ohio Bureau of Investigation recalled the day he showed Snook two Colt .38-caliber detective special revolvers he had just purchased. "I had brought them to the range to try them out," he said, "but I was unable to groove my shots, which scattered like shrapnel." Yantis suspected the revolvers might be faulty. Snook asked

---

[3] The .38-caliber, single-shot Scheutzen rifle was used only for target shooting.

to give them a try. Taking one gun in each hand, the professor began rapid-fire at the bull's-eye. "When he finished," Yantis said, "a quarter would have covered the holes in the target."

Ray Bracken already was at the New York Central Railroad range on Fisher Road when Snook pulled up in his pride and joy, a blue 1929 Ford coupe recently purchased for $600. It had fewer than 1,350 miles on the odometer. The other three members of the Columbus civilian team arrived shortly thereafter, and together they practiced before the competition. Snook and Bracken were literally "the big guns" at the match, easily outdistancing the police officers. Bracken scored 272 points out of 300; Snook posted 264 points for second place.

A fierce and proud competitor, Snook was disappointed with his marksmanship this day. A month earlier, in competition with 24 other Ohio shooters, including Bracken, he had won the match with an outstanding score of 348 points out of 350. He knew he had to sharpen his eye-hand coordination, which only could be achieved through constant practice. Still, such was his reputation as a world champion that members of the police division team extracted a promise from him to coach them in rapid-fire pistol shooting.

Little did Snook suspect, however, that he would be back at that same shooting range two days later when that chapter of his life, like the Ohio State graduates, would pass into history.

2 | 'WE JUST SEEN IT!'

"There's a woman's body over there in the weeds! Hey, mister! There's a body over there!"

Ephriam Johnson, busy plowing a two-acre, sweet-corn patch with his two-horse team, couldn't hear at first what the two boys running toward him were yelling. A body? In the weeds? Finally, they got close enough and breathlessly repeated their message: "There's a body over there in the weeds! We just seen it!"

Johnson dropped the reins and hastened to the scene of the discovery. Sure enough. A woman's body. Bloody and disheveled. Sprawled face down in weeds of timothy, whitetop, and clover. In one hand a linen handkerchief, stained by blood.

"Lordy!" Johnson said softly.

The two North High School chums, Paul "Krummy" Krumlauf and Milton Miller, were visiting the New York Central Railroad rifle range for the first time. It was June 14, a pleasant but cool morning, and the Columbus school year had ended two days earlier. Each had a rifle to fire but before taking the weapons out of the car, they noticed the farmer in the field about 200 yards away. Fearing a ricochet might endanger the man, the boys thought it best to warn him they would be shooting in the area. As they walked toward him, they made their gruesome discovery, initiating the most celebrated case of murder in the capital city's history.

The 76-year-old dirt farmer agreed to stay put while the boys, both 16, fetched the police. They jumped into Miller's Whippet Four sedan – actually it was his father's car – and headed for Columbus police headquarters at Sullivant and McDowell avenues, a distance of less than six miles.[4] However, it would be an hour and a half before they returned in a police car with two officers, Corporal John B. May and Patrol Officer Emmett Cloud.

In the interval, Johnson had left his post to return his horses to the barn about a quarter-mile away on McKinley Avenue. By the time he returned to the scene, a gaggle of curious men, women and children had gathered. Viewing the position of the body again, Johnson realized that half of it lay on ground he had mowed the day before, on June 13. "No," he told an onlooker, stating the obvious, "she wasn't there when I mowed."

May and Cloud moved the spectators back a few feet from the body, then made a preliminary examination to determine that the woman was, in fact, dead. Both officers hurried to a nearby home for a telephone to summon the Franklin County coroner, Dr. Joseph A. Murphy, and police photographer Homer C. Richter.

Before the coroner arrived, John W. Guy and Ralph Paul, Franklin County deputy sheriffs who regularly patrolled the area, pulled into the rifle range. Guy had been on Fisher Road shortly before 10 the previous evening, having just given a motorist a ticket at Hague Avenue and Skidmore Road, less than a mile away. That was at 9:50 p.m. From there he patrolled past the range, "looking for chicken thieves," he said, but observed nothing unusual. The range was well-shaded and black as black can be during the heavy downpour that began about 30 minutes earlier.

---

[4] The Old Workhouse at Sullivant and McDowell avenues served as a temporary police headquarters and city prison following a fire at City Hall in 1920.

Dr. Murphy, the veteran coroner who had held the post for 13 years, was at home when he received Cloud's phone call. By the time he arrived at the range, the crowd had swelled to nearly 20, and the Columbus and Franklin County officers had made their own initial investigations. For instance, Guy had noticed on the victim's left wrist a man's watch missing its crystal and stopped at 10 o'clock. When he lifted the wrist for a closer look, the watch started to run again.

It was Dr. Murphy, however, who turned the body over and discovered the horrific, multiple wounds. The victim's nose had been flattened. Gripping it with his thumb and forefinger, he jiggled it back into shape. The woman's right hand still grasped the soiled handkerchief; the left hand held a few strands of long hair. Taking his handkerchief from his pocket, he wiped caked blood from the face as well as he could and sent the body to the Glenn L. Myers Mortuary on Second Avenue for further examination.

Initially the police thought that the victim had been murdered elsewhere and dumped at the range, although there was nothing definitive in the evidence to substantiate that conclusion. The bigger issue was the identity of the woman and, of course, who killed her. Columbus Chief of Police Harry E. French assigned his best officers to the case, including Chief of Detectives Wilson G. "Shelly" Shellenbarger and detectives Otto Warren Phillips, Robert McCall and Larry Van Skaik. Franklin County Prosecutor John J. Chester Jr. assigned county Detective Howard Lavely and two officers, Deputy Sheriffs Paul and Guy. Until the victim was identified, however, there was little to go on other than physical evidence from the crime scene.

The two boys and farmer Johnson were first to be questioned, but they had nothing of value to add. Neither did residents in the sparsely populated area. Most paid little attention to noise in the vicinity of the range, having heard shots so often. Officers spoke to several members of the Columbus Businessmen's Rifle Club who had been practicing at the range until about 8 p.m. They had been identified by Robert W. Anderson, manager of the range, who also saw Dr. Snook practicing on the firing line in the afternoon, trying out some new ammunition.

A search of the area where the body was found turned up a few items that appeared linked to the crime, the most important of which was a set of 12 keys, including one for a safety deposit box. The investigation extended along McKinley Avenue to several abandoned stone quarries nearby, but they yielded no clues.

The following day, Saturday, more than 1,000 curiosity seekers – some carrying infants in their arms – visited the grounds of the rifle range. Neighborhood farmer Lincoln Burwell said the number seemed to him to be more than 5,000. They were drawn there by word-of-mouth and a one-paragraph article in *The Columbus Citizen*. "Police were called Friday afternoon," it said, "to the rifle range in Fisher Rd. near McKinley Ave., where the body of a woman was found by boys. An arm was said to be missing. Coroner Murphy was called." In fact, both arms were attached to the torso.

The multitudes trampled the grass and weeds for 150 feet around at the same time the police were still conducting their investigation. Detective Van Skaik even had city prison trusties searching the grounds in an effort to get to the evidence before the crowd did. People clambered over the stone wall along Fisher Road, knocking loose the stones. For souvenirs, they swiped stakes that marked where the body and certain items of evidence, such as the keys, were found.

Burwell, enjoying the spotlight, described Fisher Road as "a lover's lane."

"There wasn't a night that three or four cars weren't parked here in the shadows," he told a reporter. "Girls are not going to let their fellows take them where another girl had her throat cut by her fellow. Thinking about it wouldn't make for kissing."

Late in the afternoon police received their first break in the case. Two sisters, Alice and Beatrice Bustin, telephoned police to report that their roommate, Theora K. Hix, had not returned from a date the night before. Like Alice, Theora was a premed student in her second year. For 10 months, the three women had shared a one-bedroom apartment above J. T. Cummings' State Drug & Supply Shoppe, at 1658 Neil Avenue, on the edge of the Ohio State University campus.

"We thought nothing of it when she did not come in until late, but Thursday night was the first time she did not appear before morning," Beatrice said. Because of the heavy downpour, the women thought Theora might have decided to spend the night with a family for whom she had been a baby sitter.

It was 4:45 p.m. Friday when Mrs. Helen Custer, record clerk at the city prison, took the telephone call from Alice Bustin. Mrs. Custer soon realized that the missing girl might be the one found at the rifle range. She called the sisters back. "Go to the Glenn Myers undertaking establishment on Second Avenue and perhaps you will find your friend," she told them. They did so, but neither young woman was prepared for what they saw: the lifeless body of their roommate, battered about the head almost beyond recognition. Positive identification was made from the clothing they had seen Theora lay out on her bed the evening before.[5]

The women told police that Theora had been in good spirits as she prepared to go out. She had worked until 5 p.m. as a secretary-typist in the office of Dean William McPherson, the 60-year-old chemistry professor and head of the Graduate School at Ohio State University.

After bathing, she slipped on a new light, blue garter belt to hold up her light-gray silk stockings. The Bustin girls also identified for police their roommate's combination suit (one-piece bra and bloomers that fastened up the left side), black slippers, and a dark brown silk crepe dress with a collar and belt. Virtually every item was now stained with mud and blood. They noted that the small black purse adorned with a green ornament that she carried was not among the effects. Could it have been a robbery gone terribly awry?

The sisters remembered the purse in particular because the three of them had laughed about it. "I've got to empty this thing before too long," Theora had said. "It is chock-full of a lot of letters and papers of absolutely no account." And off she went.

---

[5] The Bustin sisters shared one bed; Theora had the other.

As word of the murder spread and Theora's photograph appeared in the local newspapers, more citizens came forward with information. Alice Bustin remembered that she had received a telephone call from a woman asking for Theora, claiming she had a luncheon date with the missing woman Friday at OSU's Pomerene Hall. It later was established that the caller was Peggy Edwards, secretary to Esther Allen Gaw, dean of women at the university. Edwards, one of Theora's few close friends, professed to be as mystified as anyone by her friend's nonappearance and could add nothing of value for the police. "Miss Hix never spoke to me about her friends," Edwards said. "I am sure she wasn't picked up. She didn't associate much with others, and she never flirted."

Police also heard from taxi driver Earl Nichols. He remembered picking up a "very nervous" young woman on campus about 7 p.m. Thursday and driving her to the Hilltop in the western part of the city. On the way, the woman asked for and received three cigarettes from Nichols, chain-smoking each one only partially. She told him she was looking for "a man in a coupe. Go the back way," she instructed. "Cut through the quarries, because the party I am looking for comes in the back way in his coupe."

When they neared the State Hospital for the Insane, she had him wait while she left the taxi for about 10 minutes. Then he drove her back to the university area, the woman smoking two more of his cigarettes on the way. "She was fidgety about something," Nichols said. He dropped her off at Neil Avenue and 10th Street. The following day Nichols turned up at the Myers mortuary to identify the body, as did Mrs. Alice Moran, an acquaintance of Theora's and secretary of the Neil House dormitory.

Mark Lonnis, a counterman at The Clock restaurant, a popular downtown dining establishment at 161 N. High St., remembered Theora as a frequent patron – two or three times a week – in the company of an older man.

Not so forthcoming was William McPherson, dean of the Graduate School who 10 years later would become for the second time acting president of OSU.[6] He knew Theora. Two days before the murder, he had hired her as a stenographer in his office. Curiously, however, for almost 24 hours following the discovery of the body he refused to answer the telephone or come to the door of his residence to talk with police. Finally, while in pajamas, McPherson stuck his head out of a second-story bedroom window to deny to police standing below that he knew the woman. Later he would recall who she was.

McPherson was one of many associated with the university contacted by police after they knew from the Bustin sisters that Theora was a medical student and worked part time on campus. Bertha Dillon, telephone operator at University Hospital, was among the first contacted by police. She saw Theora Thursday night because Dillon was to train the young woman as a summer relief telephone operator. Theora arrived at the switchboard shortly after 6:30 p.m. but left about an hour later, saying that she had to keep a date. "I'll be back about 9:30 or 10," she promised.

"She was very quiet and seemed nervous about something," Dillon recalled. "She didn't talk much and told me nothing about herself. She was to have started work Saturday night as a relief operator between 6 p.m. and 9 p.m."

Until cabbie Nichols came forward, police thought that Dillon was the last to have seen Theora alive. But then they began to pick up information that the young woman had been seen a number of times in the company of an older man who drove a navy blue coupe. It was a fresh and promising lead for police.

Friday evening, police notified Dr. and Mrs. Melvin Hix of Bradenton, Florida, that their daughter had been murdered. Before moving to Florida in 1923 and becoming associated with the University of Florida, Dr. Hix taught music for 20 years at the Horace Mann School for Girls, a private school associated with Teachers College at Columbia University in New York City.

---

[6] In 1924 McPherson was professor of chemistry, dean of the Graduate School and acting president of Ohio State.

While Hix made plans to travel by train to Columbus, a 2 ½ day journey, Dr. Snook sat in his living room, reading *The Ohio State Journal Night Green*. "I know this girl who was murdered," he told his wife casually. "She was a stenographer in our office."

"It was a horrible deed," Helen Snook agreed. "Just horrible. What kind of a girl was she?"

"Quiet, very quiet," her husband replied.

3 | THEORA

On a platform in a city square,
Theora Hix did stand,
And from her mouth did come
the words, "Down with man!"
All through the country she has traveled,
This city to all to make known,
For she has become a deliverer,
In woman asserting her own.
Northfield Seminary yearbook 1923

Once the coroner's assistant pulled back the sheet for the Bustin sisters, revealing a woman's battered head, the mystery surrounding the identity of the murder victim on the rifle range ended. Still, police wanted to know who was Theora Katherine Hix? Who did she associate with and who killed her?

First questioned were the Bustin girls, of course, but they knew little about their roommate, although they believed she had had good breeding. The sisters found her to be somewhat secretive about her occasional dates and others with whom she associated. "We have known only of one man that Theora had dated, and we met him only once," Beatrice told police. "His name is Marion Meyers. But as far as we know, Theora had not seen him for a few months." However, the sisters were able to direct police to Theora's parents in Florida, Dr. and Mrs. Melvin Hix.

Theora's parents had been married for 20 years before their first and only child was born in Flushing, New York, on August 10, 1904. Both parents, children of the Victorian Age, were raised in cages of conformity – corsets, covered limbs and choking collars, for example. They had experienced a "proper" patriarchal upbringing that included the subservience of the wife-mother figure. Young ladies didn't work to earn a living. Now, in the "anything goes" Roaring 20s, parents worried about their offspring advancing to adulthood in a world of smoky speakeasies, mobster mania, bathtub gin and gaily painted Bohemians living on the other side of life. The world no longer moved as slowly as a horse and carriage. For parents such as Dr. and Mrs. Hix, it seemed to be spiraling out of control.

Before retiring on a pension in 1923 to Florida where he became associated with the University of Florida, Dr. Hix taught music at the Horace Mann School in New York. The family lived frugally but comfortably at 115 Delaware Ave., Flushing, Queens, a borough of New York City. Although money was scarce, the family managed, until illness to both parents depleted their resources. The Hixes were forced to tell their daughter that they would finance her college education but would be unable to afford medical-school expenses.

"That's all right, Dad," Theora had said. "I don't expect you to. I want to earn some of my own money, and I would like to take a course in a business school before I go to college."

Theora's mother was a quiet woman, with graying hair. Often dressed in white, she resembled a Norman Rockwell painting, motherly and quaint. You could imagine her in an apron, bringing the Thanksgiving turkey to the table on a cobalt-blue Willowware platter. She was the keeper of the small household, and her Bible guided her in the rearing of her child.

Hix had been teaching Latin and Greek when his daughter was born. His multilingual background was the influence in her distinctive name. The couple chose Theora, meaning "God-given." After 20 years of a childless marriage and because of their religious convictions, the choice for their baby's name was undoubtedly a testament to their feelings. Her father preferred to use the nickname he gave her: "Thee."

There had been nothing unusual about Theora's childhood. She attended Public School 20 in Flushing, then Flushing High School in Queens. She was attractive and bright, advancing rapidly socially and scholastically. Because her parents desired that she have "in every respect, the moral and religious influences," they sent her to the Northfield Seminary for Young Ladies in East Northfield, Massachusetts, for her senior year in high school. It was founded in 1879 by Dwight Lyman Moody, a Protestant evangelist. At graduation, teachers cited Theora for her ability and character and as one who had an "amount of impeccable countenance."

Her fellow classmates, writing in the senior yearbook, found "Teddy" – a nickname given to her by her classmates that her father resented as undignified – to be "quiet and unassuming." She had "many campus friends who would be glad to have her nearer." On the other hand, it was noted that on occasion she "waxes frisky."

Her father, now 64, proudly recalled that "she had been asked to act as a kind of monitor or chaperone in her house (dorm). When girls wanted to go shopping, they were told by the dorm heads that they could go if Theora Hix would go with them." Her teacher and student friends said "she was trusted as no other girl in the house was trusted."

Before entering Ohio State University in the spring of 1924, Theora attended business school in New York City, becoming an accomplished stenographer and typist. She also took a position with an art firm but stayed there only a few months. In the fall of 1923, she spent time in Florida to care for her mother, who suffered "health problems." She returned to Florida for the Christmas holidays to help her father with the housekeeping.

Her father was happy knowing Theora would pursue her education in Columbus because it would be "a safer place for girls than any other university town that we know." Also, Mrs. Hix had a sister, Mrs. Harriet Holmes, who lived two blocks from the OSU campus. In the spring of 1924, Theora lived with her for a short time until she found student housing. Still, her aunt would look in on her niece now and then, which she did until she also moved to the Sunshine State for her health.

Between quarters and during holidays, Theora joined her parents in Florida. In the summer of 1926, Dr. and Mrs. Hix motored to Columbus to visit Theora, and the following summer the family met in Knoxville, Tennessee, to take a motor car tour of North Carolina and Tennessee.

"In all her visits and in all her letters, there never was a sign of any mental disturbance or of any anxiety or trouble," her father said.

Hix, however, worried about one particular quality in his daughter. "She was fearless. I do not think she knew the meaning of the word *fear*."

He warned her: "Look out for the man who tries to induce you to do anything wrong and at the same time tells you he loves you. If you go wrong with a man, you'll be sorry all the rest of your life. Look out for the flattery of men, my daughter."

A classmate from the seminary attested to Theora's dislike for men at that time. "When we had a party, it was always necessary to make a blind date for Theora," the girl said. "She never wanted to go with the same man twice. She was one of the school's most popular girls and a real athlete. She was a tennis champion and also played golf and basketball."

The yearly *Who's Who* published by the seminary listed Theora as "the most bashful girl." Theora wrote the class history and was prominent in all activities but begged to be left out when it came to dating.

Under her class picture is stated simply, "Good nature and good sense are never separated," and that a "steadfastness of character and her loyalty of spirit have attributed much in upholding the standards of Northfield."

Theora had a certain pride in her command of things. Her aims were high. By the end of high school she knew she wanted to pursue a medical career – and she pursued her goal through various jobs and other financial assistance to pay for her education.

Although she was an average student at Ohio State, she had been all her parents could want, and they were proud of her achievements. In another week or so, Theora would have taken her examinations for her second year in medical school.

Her parents didn't know her to flirt with the fraternity men who wore the raccoon coats and drove the noisy "flivvers" around the university. She didn't have many friends on the campus who met her for coffee or went with her to the movies. Most found her to be "reserved and moody." Her energies seemingly took aim toward her future – her success.

During their sad trip to Columbus by train, Dr. and Mrs. Hix purchased a copy of every newspaper available along the route. Virtually every one had the story of the murdered coed from Ohio State.

"My daughter couldn't have changed so much practically overnight," he said, but he admitted she was lonely in Columbus. "I have only one thing to live for: to see that this fiend (Theora's killer) gets his due punishment."

4 | THE ACCUSED

"Identify This Man; Solve Hix Mystery!" *The Ohio State Journal* urged its readers a day after the body was found.

"Somewhere in Columbus there is a man who is heavily built, wears horn-rimmed glasses, is about 40 years old and drives a Model T Ford coupe," the Saturday newspaper said. "If you know of such a man, you may hasten the solution of one of the most gruesome crimes in the history of Columbus by informing police of your knowledge or suspicions."

By Saturday, a demure portrait of Theora appeared in the local newspapers, giving rise to additional tips from the public. Out-of-town newspapers, including *The New York Times*, began to follow the story in some detail. Within three more days, the incredible case of the coed and the killer would command front-page attention across the land.

When *The Columbus Evening Dispatch* rolled off the presses Saturday afternoon, photographs of two suspects in custody commanded the front page.

Marion T. Meyers, the 36-year-old head of the Ohio Corn Borer[7] Research Bureau at OSU's College of Agriculture, was one of them. At

---

[7] The corn borer is a moth that infests and damages corn crops.

the highly unusual hour of 3:15 Saturday morning, he had made an anonymous call to Columbus police from his home in Bono, in northeast Ohio, to inquire about "Miss Hix." A Gamma Alpha fraternity brother and graduate student, Robert K. Summerbell, had telephoned Meyers from Columbus to report that Theora's picture was in the newspapers because she had been murdered. At first Meyers thought Summerbell was playing a joke on him, so when the police operator tried to get Meyers to give his name, he hung up.

There was a reason for his call. On numerous occasions over two years, Theora and Meyers had dated; in fact, he had proposed marriage, only to be rejected. She wanted to wait until she had graduated from medical school. In recent months, however, they had seen each other but not dated, primarily because he now was engaged to Eleanor Ricker from Wooster, Ohio. In fact, they were planning their wedding and honeymoon.

Realizing that Summerbell's call was no joke, Meyers wasted little time getting to Columbus, driving through the dawn. Upon arrival he visited the Myer funeral parlor, speaking briefly there with Coroner Murphy, who had just completed his preliminary autopsy.

"Her throat was cut in such a manner that the jugular vein and another vein were severed, indicating that someone had wielded the knife who knew just what veins should be slit in order that the wound would be fatal," the doctor told reporters. He added that she also had been severely beaten, with a hammer, evidently.

Later Saturday morning, police took Meyers into custody at the fraternity house, 1501 Neil Avenue.

At about the same time, Detective Larry F. Van Skaik knocked on the door of Snook's home, observed by two reporters – James Fusco of *The Columbus Citizen* and Garland Hick of United Press. From their parked car, the newsmen watched as the professor stepped out on the front porch, neatly dressed in a gray wool suit, but he had yet to put on his jacket and tie. His right hand was bandaged and cradled in a sling. He had injured it midweek while working on his car, he explained.

"Do you know Miss Hix?" asked Van Skaik.

"For quite some time," Snook answered. "For quite some time."

"I'd like you to come with me to police headquarters, professor," Van Skaik said pleasantly, explaining that it would be helpful to the investigation.

"Is it necessary?" The officer said it was.

"Would it be all right if I had my breakfast first?" Snook asked. Van Skaik said that it would be "if you think it is best for me to tell your wife what I want you for." Snook hesitated, then agreed to get breakfast downtown instead. They stopped at the Geis Restaurant on West Broad Street for doughnuts and coffee.

It was not the usual way to take a man in for questioning, but at this stage in the investigation there was nothing that specifically linked Snook to the crime. Van Skaik even allowed Snook to drive his own car, accompanied by the detective, but Snook was somewhat annoyed. He had been looking forward to driving the family to South Lebanon Saturday afternoon to spend a few days with his 73-year-old mother. Sunday was Father's Day.

After a congenial breakfast, the two men went to police headquarters and the office of the chief of detectives, Wilson G. "Shelly" Shellenbarger. Police impounded Snook's car, although he was unaware of that fact at the time. Police physician Woodrow C. Pickering took a look at Snook's hand, which had been dressed the night before by Dr. Richard Good at University Hospital. Pickering noted that the wound appeared to be more than 24 hours old.

Also unbeknownst to the professor, his wife, Helen, had visitors Saturday afternoon – the police. Officers came to her door with a search warrant in hand and looked for evidence of foul play. Most curious were the embers they found in the furnace despite the warmth of the day. "From trash I burned," Helen explained. In addition to the ashes, police took as evidence two suits recently cleaned, a stained shirt, a felt fedora, also stained, and a pocketknife with a smudge on it. From Snook's automobile, they recovered a pair of men's gloves, a ball-peen hammer, several hairpins and strands of light-brown hair and a woman's umbrella.

Back at police headquarters, the tall, balding and somewhat high-strung, Meyers underwent questioning. He told detectives he had been at the fraternity house the evening of the murder, leaving only briefly to mail some letters. Friday morning he left Columbus early to drive the 135 miles north to Bono. Several fraternity brothers confirmed his story.

Snook, calm and professorial, admitted to knowing both Theora and Meyers. Because she promised to do some typing for him while he worked on a book, the professor recently had taken her on an automobile ride to describe the details to her. Theora mentioned her concern for her safety living in Columbus, so he gave her a small pistol for her protection. Snook owned a number of firearms.

As for the night of the murder, Snook explained that until 8 p.m. or so, he worked on a manuscript in his office in the Veterinary Clinic Building. Veterinary school night watchman Harrison B. "Dick" Case would confirm that, he said. Before heading home, however, the professor drove to the Scioto Country Club to pick up a pair of shooting glasses he had left in his locker, returned to High Street to buy a newspaper and arrived home shortly before 9:30 p.m. His wife, Helen, would confirm that she saw him eating a sandwich at the dining table. Concerned about the heavy rain, she had left her bed, descended the stairs in slippers and robe and closed the kitchen window.

After several hours of questioning, police decided to hold both men without specific charges and without bond, although they believed Meyers to be their man. Snook retained as his attorney former Municipal Court Judge John F. Seidel, whom he had known for 20 years, and Seidel's law partner, Ernest O. Ricketts, of Ricketts & Seidel. Around the courthouse, Ricketts was known as "Roaring Ricketts" for his boisterous courtroom mannerisms. Meyers hired D. N. Postlewaite and John W. Bricker, who would become governor of Ohio and a United States senator.

Snook gave up very little information, playing a cat–and–mouse game with his interrogators. Then he clammed up, insisting that he be allowed to see his attorneys. His counsel had not been permitted to visit, prompting Ricketts to file with Common Pleas Judge Dana F. Reynolds a writ of mandamus, commanding authorities to grant Snook the right to legal counsel.

Meanwhile, police stalled for time, awaiting the return to the city Sunday afternoon of Franklin County's "boy prosecutor," John J. Chester Jr. What awaited him had all the earmarks of a high-profile case, and the 31-year-old attorney intended to make the most of it. Already the talk about town was that Chester could be a judge, congressman, United States senator and even president of the United States. Chester's reaction: "Well, I never thought of being president."

But all that would have to wait this day. He rode horseback in the morning and then served as luncheon host to the entire Columbus City Council.

The probe continued, attributable in large measure to the many people who came forward Saturday after seeing the photographs in the newspapers. Landlady Mrs. Margaret M. Smalley did so. She and her husband rented rooms at their home, a three-story, brick rooming house at 24 W. Hubbard Avenue. On February 11, she told police, she had rented a third-floor room to a Mr. Snook. A brass bed, dresser, stove, small settee and two rocking chairs all but filled the unimaginatively decorated, drab room. Residents shared the toilet down the hall. The rent was $4 a week – in cash.

"I think this is what I am looking for," Snook had said on his first visit. "It seems to be a very nice room. I shall come back Wednesday night to take it. It is for my wife and me," he said. "Both of us demonstrate salts[8] and will not be in the room much. We are from Newark" – the birthplace of Snook's wife.

About two months later, Snook moved to Room 6 on the second floor of the annex, in the rear, away from the street. It cost a dollar less, which pleased tightfisted Snook to no end. Mrs. Smalley said she rarely saw the couple because they entered and, after two or three hours, left by the rear. She only had one brief encounter with Theora, who identified herself as Mrs. Snook.

---

[8] Salt sales representatives.

After police heard Mrs. Smalley's story, they brought her to the city prison, where she confronted Snook in the jail corridor.

"Good evening, Mr. Snook."

"Good evening," he replied, calmly.

"Have you ever seen this woman before?" asked Detective Otto W. Phillips.

"Yes. I rented a room from her last February for Miss Hix and myself and kept it until yesterday (Friday, June 14)." He had told Mrs. Smalley that he had been transferred to Washington Court House and would no longer need the room. He returned two keys to her.

"I was so disappointed about his leaving that I grumbled about it all the evening," the landlady later commented, "but he left both keys in the room."

After the confrontation, Snook admitted that he had used the room several times for a rendezvous with Theora. The "love nest," as the newspapers called it, now became known, as did Snook's illicit affair with a coed. Many in the community were shocked by the revelation.

Mrs. Freda Bowen also telephoned police. She recalled that about Friday noontime Snook came into the Brown Dye House, 1100 N. High St., and dropped off an old gray suit to be cleaned so he could wear it over the weekend at the family farm. "Will you make it a hurry order?" he asked her.

"When would you like it back?"

"Tomorrow noon, if possible," Snook replied.

Later in the day Newton Fisher, a worker at the dry cleaners, would discover what appeared to be bloodstains on the lining of both sleeves, on a pant leg and on both knees. The suit was given to police for further examination.

Yet another informant who contacted police was Charles Lang, night watchman at the YWCA on S. 4th Street Before moving in with the Bustin sisters, Theora lived on campus in Mack Hall, then at the Y. Lang said he remembered Snook as the gentleman who frequently brought her back between midnight and 2 a.m. He said she would ask him to say nothing about her late hours, and for his silence Snook would tip him 25 cents.[9] Lang readily picked the professor out of a lineup at the police station.

Early Sunday morning, Shellenbarger, accompanied by detectives Otto W. Phillips and Robert McCall, drove Snook to the scene of the crime, New York Central Railroad rifle range. Two-and-two were starting to add up for police: Snook was the only one in custody who knew both Theora and the location of the range. As they walked through the ankle-high weeds and grass, Snook shuddered slightly but remained calm – icy calm, one might say.

"Have you ever been out here before?" asked Phillips.

"Yes, once or twice," Snook replied. He showed no recognition of anything there, however, and the group moved on, passing the Scioto Country Club, the veterinary school and the love nest on High Street. After more than an hour of touring, the officers returned the professor to the county jail.

It was a devastatingly sad Father's Day for Dr. Hix, who arrived from Florida with his wife at 12:55 p.m. Met by Columbus detectives at Union Station in downtown Columbus, Hix immediately went to a newsstand to pick up the local newspapers. An editorial-page cartoon in *The Ohio State Sunday Journal* caught his eye. It depicted a hairy fiend hovering over the body of a girl, bloody knife in hand. The caption read, "The worst of the brute that is left in our civilization."

The elderly couple went to the home of Mrs. Minton F. Rowe, a church secretary and friend of the family, and there spoke to Columbus police. In the evening, the couple visited the Myers funeral parlor for some quiet, private time with their daughter.

The establishment was anything but quiet a few hours earlier. It had to close its doors after several thousand had paraded through the parlors to see Theora's bludgeoned body laid out in a polished mahogany coffin. Some were disappointed, perhaps, for the undertakers had done their work well. The blows to the head and face were all but invisible.

---

[9] About $3 when adjusted for inflation in 2008.

A similar stream of onlookers drove past the Snook home on 10th Avenue. Inside, a small circle of close friends, including the Rev. Isaac E. Miller of the King Avenue church where the Snooks were married, comforted Helen Snook and her daughter. By Sunday afternoon, Mrs. Snook had moved to the home of a friend to avoid the curious passersby.

On Monday morning, Chester again took charge of the questioning of the two suspects, and again he denied their attorneys private access to their clients until Ricketts produced the writ. Even then, Chester allowed the suspects very little private time with their lawyers. Ricketts made it clear to the prosecutor that if charges were not filed forthwith, he would seek a writ of habeas corpus[10] to secure his client's release.

Chester put the Franklin County Grand Jury, which met every Monday, on standby. He led it to believe that he would request a first-degree murder indictment that afternoon, but he did not have the confession he sought. With each passing hour, it appeared most likely that it would be Snook, not Meyers, who would be indicted. In fact, Shellenbarger told reporters that unless more evidence surfaced, Meyers would be released within 24 hours. Already Chester was pushing the 48 hours that a suspect could be held without formal charges.

Snook received bad, although not unexpected, news Monday afternoon. After conferring with Dr. Oscar V. Brumley, acting dean of the veterinary college, Ohio State University President Dr. George W. Rightmire dismissed Snook from the faculty.

"The connection of Dr. James H. Snook as professor of veterinary medicine at Ohio State University is herewith terminated in view of his admission of his moral delinquencies, which have had sufficient verification," Rightmire announced. Two days later, Meyers was similarly dismissed for a lack of moral judgment.

In a personal letter to Snook, the president said the dismissal was "my painful duty ... (and) a cause of sincere regret." He also wrote Theora's parents, stating how "inexpressibly shocked" he was. "If we

---

[10] A legal action to secure the release of an individual in custody.

had had earlier information about the conduct included in Dr. Snook's admissions, the university would have taken action at that time. No employee of the university will be shielded for one moment...when facts showing his moral delinquency are established."

The many members of the alumni and faculty who expressed concern for the damage the adverse publicity was having on the university spurred Rightmire to action. In an editorial the day after the president's announcement, *The Ohio State Journal* noted, "Some horrified parents of girls and boys no doubt will decide to send their children to some institution on which no such shadow has fallen." On the other hand, there were bound to be "a few undesirables" on a campus with 14,000 students and a teaching staff of 1,200, the newspaper said, "but the moral atmosphere at Ohio State University is good."

The *Logan* (Ohio) *Republican* wasn't so sure. Its editorial June 18 stated: "Ohio State University is partly responsible for the untimely death of another of our students... What are we coming to when the daughters who were sent to a state institution to be educated are made the victims of the animal passions of some lecherous professor? ... It is the opinion of everybody with whom we have talked on the matter that the university needs a general cleaning up and weeding out."Monday evening, some 60 hours after Snook's arrest, Helen visited her husband in jail for the first time, along with his attorneys. It was a tearful reunion.

"Mrs. Snook is convinced of her husband's complete innocence and she is for him," Seidel told reporters eager for a comment. "Neither Doctor nor Mrs. Snook are involved in the murder."

The attorney could cite no motive for Snook committing murder. "After talking to him today, I am convinced that there was no rift between him and the Hix girl. They had a perfect understanding. They were to have an even more happy relationship this summer. As soon as he came back from a short vacation trip, she was to become his stenographer. They were to work together over a book. He was to share the profits with her. They were just about to enter upon a happy period of their romance. He was to rent another room later as a rendezvous. Where could there be any motive in his killing her?"

After Helen left her husband, Chester, Detective Howard Lavely and Sheriff Harry T. Paul took Snook to his office on campus. There they discovered a well-worn copy of *The Art of Love*,[11] a book that Snook had purchased for $25 – at Theora's urging.

"Every man wants to do some daring deed of sacrifice for his lady; every woman desires to undergo some penance, to accomplish some act of complete renunciation, for her man," the author, Walter Franklin Robie, writes. He frequently wrote in this genre, handing out intimate advice to *married* couples. In *The Art of Love*, Robie discussed such salacious subjects as kissing, orgasms, homosexuality, frigidity and titillating the breasts. Even for the Roaring '20s, it was wicked reading.

Snook mentioned to Lavely that the book was very rare and hard to obtain. "Get a copy of it and read up on it," he urged.

Police also found an accumulation of erotic literature and obscene poetry and a love letter from an unidentified former sweetheart. Apparently Theora was not the only one with whom the veterinarian had had an affair.

In Snook's locker at the country club, police found what *The New York Daily News* described as "medical capsules designed to awake dormant emotions, bottles of ether and other lulling drugs and code messages in the dead languages that when deciphered proved instructions for exotic living." A campus "love-dope cult" was under investigation, the newspaper said, intimating that Snook trafficked in dope on campus. None of it proved to be true.

At midnight, Chester, Dr. James Quinn Dorgan, a psychiatrist, and Detective Lavely quietly took the despondent Meyers from his cell to view Theora's body at the funeral home. Chester wanted to make sure Meyers was not his man before releasing him. Viewing the body left the corn-borer expert visibly shaken by what he saw. In Dr. Dorgan's opinion, Meyers could not be the killer. Thus, he no longer was a

---

[11] Robie, William Franklin: Boston, R. G. Badger 1921.

suspect, although another day would pass before he walked out of prison.

Mrs. Snook arrived for questioning at the prison Tuesday, having run the gauntlet of reporters waiting outside her home. She became angry at their repeated questions, and all but one went unanswered: She said she did not know of her husband's affair.

Russell Rebrassier, an assistant professor at the veterinary school, accompanied her, steadying her by the arm. She appeared very prim and proper in a white dress, hat and shoes – perfect attire for church. Surely she did not expect what awaited her.

Attorney Edwin J. Schanfarber met Mrs. Snook at the city prison. She had retained him after Chester denied Seidel access to the interview room, revealing the deepening animosity between the defense and the young prosecutor. Chester seethed still at having to bow to the court order earlier that gave Seidel and Ricketts access to Snook. Even so, Schanfarber had but a short time with Helen.

For nearly five hours Chester, Schellenbarger and Chief of Police Harry E. French pounded Snook's distraught wife with questions. Tears flowed much of the time, and at one point she became hysterical, swooned and collapsed. A policewoman and a stenographer rushed into the room with glasses of water. One described Mrs. Snook as "in a bad way." Her personal physician, Dr. John M. Thomas, was summoned to the room.

Beside herself, Helen finally corrected her story, admitting that after visiting friends, she had returned home about 8:30 p.m. Thursday and sat down to read a book in the living room. An hour or so later, a friend and neighbor, John B. Sparrow and his daughter, dropped by, seeking the name of a boy he wanted to do some work for him. He did not see Dr. Snook. When Sparrow left, Helen went upstairs to her bedroom.

It was about 10 p.m., she thought, that she heard the screen door slam and assumed her husband was home. The heavy rainstorm got her attention next, and she came downstairs in slippers and robe to close a window. Her husband sat silently, eating a sandwich.

She insisted she knew nothing about her husband's love affair until she read about the love nest in the newspapers. It later came out that all had not been well between the couple. A former boarder in the Snook home, Dwight Palmer, overheard the Snooks arguing about a divorce in April, two months earlier.

When police completed their questioning, Schanfarber spirited away the distressed housewife in his automobile. Standing on the curb, silently watching her go, was Dr. Hix.

Snook continued to spin tales for reporters visiting him in jail, claiming that Theora might have been done in by a "sheik motorist."

"She enjoyed auto rides," he said. "I often cautioned her against accepting rides from strangers…I knew of one ride she took and had to scrap to get out of it. She was lonely under certain conditions and might have taken a ride."

Snook described his relationship with the coed as "a damn fool silly love affair." He admitted she was a "good companion…very nice and dignified. She would rather talk than fight." Never was their talk of marriage, he said. "Once she told me she would not marry me on a bet."

There was a ring of truth to Theora's concern for her safety on campus. A week before the murder, she filed a complaint with OSU campus police that a stranger stalked her as she walked along 11th Avenue to where she lived with the Bustin sisters. She said the man had made an indecent proposal in the presence of the Bustin girls. She gave campus Officers Hollis Brown and Charles Kalb a description, but no arrests were made.

Late Tuesday night, coroner Murphy ruled that the Theora had died from a hemorrhage that occurred after her throat was slashed. Seventeen blows to her head and body were made *after* she was dead, he concluded.

At home that night, Chester opened his "fan" mail from concerned citizens. One letter came from Cal Crim, a well-known Cincinnati detective: "I wish to congratulate you for the efficient and diplomatic way you have handled your recent case, as the whole world had their eyes on Columbus." Another letter came from the Rev. Harry B. Lewis,

Chester's Sunday school teacher, who urged the prosecutor to mete out to Snook "the punishment he so manifestly deserves."

That is exactly what Chester intended to do, beginning with a relentless trampling of the professor.

5 | 'READ ALL ABOUT IT!'

On downtown street corners shortly after 4 p.m., newsboys called out the latest headline: "Extra! Extra! Read all about it! Dr. Snook confesses! Paper, mister?"

Eager readers snapped up copies of *The Columbus Evening Dispatch* at 2 cents apiece as fast as the newsboys could handle the traffic. The afternoon newspaper went to press with no less than six "Extras" Thursday, scooping its competition with the most important crime story of the decade. *The Dispatch*, locked in fierce battle for readership with two rivals, gloated over its achievement. How the confession was leaked to *The Dispatch* was revealed more than 20 years later by the famous American humorist and cartoonist, James Thurber,[12] in his book *The Thurber Album: A Collection of Pieces About People.*[13]

After more than 22 hours of intense cat-and-mouse questioning, which a determined prosecutor and a covey of police officers began at 1:30 p.m. Wednesday, Snook confessed to the murder of OSU College

---

[12] Thurber was a reporter at *The Dispatch* 1921-1924. At the time of the trial, however, he was an associate editor of *The New Yorker* magazine and co-author of the best-seller *Is Sex Necessary, or, Why You Feel the Way You Do.*

[13] See Afterword for the complete Thurber text relating to the scoop.

of Medicine sophomore Theora K. Hix because, he said, she threatened bodily harm to his wife and child. Later he recanted what he had said.

"She threatened...that she would take the life of my wife and baby" if he left her and went to visit his mother for a few days, the veterinarian said. During their squabble in the car, parked at the range, "she grabbed for the purse in which she sometimes carried a .41-caliber derringer that I had given her. In the struggle she was hit on the head with a hammer with the intent to stun her. She continued [to struggle] desperately and an increased number of blows of increasing force was necessary to stop her.

"Realizing then, no doubt, that her skull was fractured and to relieve her suffering, I severed her jugular with my pocketknife."

In his confession, recorded by court stenographer Ralph O. Brown, Snook could not bring himself to admit that he wielded the hammer. He apparently saw himself as the Good Samaritan, coming to her "rescue" by slitting her throat.

Getting a confession had not been easy, but Chester, his assistants, Paul Hicks and Myron B. Gessaman, and police officers Shellenbarger, French and Phillips – among others – took turns at trying to knock Snook off his lofty perch. One or two would take up the questioning while others would leave the room to check the facts of their investigation against the story Snook had just told. According to his best recollection, Chief French admitted that Snook was never warned that anything he might say could be used against him in a court of law.

When accused of hitting Theora on the head, Snook said, "I couldn't have. I'm right-handed," explaining that from the evidence the blow must've been struck by a left-handed person.

Several times during the interrogation bombardment, Snook threw up his arms and said, "Prove it." At one point he called his interrogators "a pack of liars." When informed that blood had been found in his car and on his suit at the cleaners Snook pooh-poohed the findings. "Let's talk about something else," he said. "I've been in this game too long. You can't tell me that anyone can take little spots of blood like that and tell if it is from an animal or human." The reality of DNA forensic evidence was decades away.

Snook often tipped back on the rear legs of his chair, putting both hands behind his head, smug and confident. Phillips pounced to unbalance the quarry. He grabbed the edge of the table and shouted in Snook's face: "If you are innocent, you resent these words of mine, and if there is one particle of man in you, you will smack my face." Snook arose from his seat and walked around the room, tears in his eyes.

Still, they pounded away nonstop at the professor's story until 6:30 a.m. Thursday. Only then, after 17 hours of questioning, did Chester agree to a break so Snook could get some breakfast. Chester telephoned Seidel: "Come on over. Snook is ready to talk," he said. Sensing victory, Chester also alerted the grand jury to be in session Friday.

Phillips, a captain in the British Army during World War I, told *The Dispatch*: "We mocked him, we laughed at him, we were sarcastic, we patted him on the back, we cajoled him, we possibly insulted him until shortly before dawn. We saw that he was breaking and soon would admit his guilt."

Seidel managed to see his client briefly at the jail. "I've often wondered what the 'third degree' could be like. Now I know," a haggard Snook maintained, but he denied having confessed. Then he was spirited away again to police headquarters. There, behind two locked doors – to an outer office and then to Chief French's office – the final assault on Snook took place. Ricketts tried to enter, demanding admission, pounding his fist on the outer door, all to no avail. Chester and the officers knew they had their man cornered – literally.

While right in Snook's face, the prosecutor screamed at him: "You have lied yourself out of every alibi you ever had! You will be indicted for first-degree murder Friday morning! Why don't you explain these things?!"

"I've been up here a long time without any sleep."

"Well, we've been working for days without any sleep," an angry but determined Chester replied.

"This drama stuff and loud talking are ridiculous," Snook said with amazing calm.

French, with a soft voice and 50 years as a police officer, took up the questioning as the "good cop." He told Snook: "By your own admission you have fastened the irons on yourself. I have known men to go to the chair on less than you have told me. These other men have been hostile towards you: I have not. You had better tell me for your own sake. If you go out on the street and ask anyone that you meet what they think of the case, seven out of 10 will believe you guilty."

"Do you really think so?" Snook said, pacing up and down now. "I want to see my lawyer."

He saw instead Detective Phillips again, who took up the questioning. "Were you out at the country club with the girl Thursday night?"

"Yes, you are right, but you are only guessing," the professor said. "I'll tell you about it later. Murder is not everything: You do not know the half of it."

Chester reentered, closing the door behind him. When the door swung open again, Chester emerged. "Now we have his story, and we can check all details against it," he said.

Snook, trembling, cheeks red and visibly upset, commented to nobody in particular: "I am sorry I can't establish my alibi any better." He admitted to being confused. McCall and Phillips returned the suspect to his cell, stopping for breakfast. Phillips casually asked how it happened that the professor had both love nest keys in his possession.

"You know where I got the key," the suspect said, parrying the question once again.

"At the body?"

"Yes."

The end to the long inquisition – longest in history for Columbus investigators – came about 7 a.m. Thursday. Exhausted, Snook broke down and cried for almost 30 minutes. Between sobs he told Chester that he wanted to "get it over with" and plead guilty to murder.

However, it would be several hours before court stenographer Brown would take down the first of several stories Snook would tell. This "verbal confession" had a "J. H. Snook" signature on a stenopad. Brown's shorthand notes translated to:

I met Theora Hix about three years ago. The friendship continued in a very intimate way ever since, inasmuch as she was a very good companion. I have been living with my wife all during this three-year period, and regard my wife very highly and respect her very much as a wife, but she lacked some of the companionship offered by Miss Hix.

During the three years that I knew Miss Hix I did assist her in many ways towards an education, but I found out it wasn't appreciated as much as I thought I should be. Our association was not a love affair in any sense of the word, but in time Miss Hix developed a more determined attitude in regard to dictating my movements, and the final culmination of this occurred on the 13th of June of this year when I met Miss Hix at the corner of 12th and High streets in the city of Columbus, Ohio, when we both got into my Ford coupe and proceeded to drive to Lane Avenue and then west out to the Fisher Road and to the Columbus rifle range of the New York Central Railroad Company, during which she remonstrated with me against leaving the city with my family for the weekend as I had previously planned to do. She threatened that if I did go that she would take the life of my wife and baby.

During this quarrel she grabbed for the purse in which she sometimes carried a .41-caliber derringer which I had given her. In the struggle she was hit on the head with a hammer with the intent to stun her. She continued desperately and an increased number of blows of increasing force was (sic) necessary to stop her. Realizing then, no doubt, that her skull was fractured and to relieve her suffering, I severed her jugular with my pocketknife. I then proceeded to pick up the things that had been scattered during the struggle and hurriedly left the scene of the struggle, leaving her body at that point.

The instrument which I used to quiet her was a hammer which was lying in the back seat of the Ford. After leaving the rifle range I then proceeded to go home, tossing the purse from the quarry bridge into the Scioto River on my way. After the struggle was over, I discovered the gun was not in the purse.

Here were 405 words that could send a man to the electric chair, but they told only part of the story.

Chester, who described the accused's motive for the killing as "weak," perceived Snook to be a tough customer, but one of the things that broke his "almost superhuman resistance" was the disparity in the stories told by Snook and his wife.

The (Cleveland) *Plain Dealer* hailed the confession as "a complete triumph" for the police and Chester, who expressed confidence that Snook's statement "will put him in the electric chair." Hoping to make political hay, the weary prosecutor promised an exclusive interview with Snook to reporters for *The Plain Dealer* and *The Columbus Citizen*. To other journalists he said: "Wait until tomorrow morning. I hope to have something for you then." Little did he know that Shellenbarger was a sieve, leaking all to *The Columbus Evening Dispatch* Editor Norman Kuehner over lunch, providing *The Dispatch* with its scoop.

Few were as interested in the news of the confession as Dr. Hix, who police allowed to silently watch the interrogation of Snook on Wednesday. He described Snook as "a moral pervert... shrewd and heartless."

"For six hours I sat and watched him while he was being questioned," the schoolteacher said. "I scarcely kept my eyes off him. I said over and over to myself, 'Snook, you are going to be punished. You did it.' My presence made him nervous. ... His confession is an immense relief to me. The dead cannot be brought back to life, but this man can be punished for the sake of other daughters."

Journalists tried in vain to gain an interview with Mrs. Snook at her home, darkened by grief. Her pastor, the Rev. Isaac E. Miller, came to the door to explain that Mrs. Snook had retired to her bed after taking an opiate her doctor prescribed to help her sleep. "She isn't allowed to see a soul, not even a friend," Miller said. "Shaken up, you know. Sorry." And he closed the door.

6 | A 'SCHOLASTIC SHYLOCK'

The ink on his signed confession hardly had time to dry before Snook, draped in a long, white cotton nightgown and stretched out on a prison cot, amended his story for two reporters gathered in his Franklin County jail cell at midnight Thursday.

He admitted to "feeling good" but tired, having been awakened from a deep sleep after hours of interrogation at police headquarters. He really didn't want to talk to them, but "they insisted on it because they wanted to know more about the confession."

A score of journalists showed up at the jail for the "press conference" arranged by Chester, but Sheriff Harry T. Paul allowed only two reporters into the cell with Snook: William E. Howells of *The (Cleveland) Plain Dealer* and James E. Fusco of *The Columbus Citizen*. Their interview, conducted under the dim light of a single 60-watt bulb in the corridor, lasted nearly an hour. (The cells had no lights.) Assistant County Prosecutor I.W. Garek, Sheriff Paul and his son, Deputy Sheriff Ralph Paul, and Deputy Sheriff Charles B. Norris stood nearby.

Without emotion, the accused once again described how he executed his lover, hitting her repeatedly with a hammer. When she fell out of the car, he attacked her on the ground.

"Her body twitched. It would not lie still," the accused said. "I didn't want to hit her on the head anymore." To stunned reporters he added:

"She had my sympathy."

So, as she twitched, Snook pulled out his pocketknife and, with all the skill of his profession, deftly slit her jugular vein, letting her blood trickle through the weeds. As he put it so succinctly, "She was still when I left."

He said the trouble began that fateful night with an argument over his intention to visit his mother for a few days at her home. It was an argument the professor and the coed had had before. Each time she insisted that he spend weekends with her. Three weeks before the murder, for example, they quarreled while out riding in the car. It was 3 a.m. before he got her out of the car.

"I was angry enough to kill her then," he admitted.

On the night of June 13, once again "she told me I mustn't go," Snook said. "She didn't say why…she had assumed to control me. I didn't like that. I decided to go to the rifle range. There we quarreled again, and she became quite loud.

"Then, as she reached for her handbag, she said, 'I'll kill you and your wife, too, and your baby!'"

The reporters scribbled furiously as Snook continued unabated, his right foot twitching continuously underneath the sheet covering his feet. "I knew she often carried a gun I had given her. She said she wanted to get out to go and kill my wife and baby.

"I don't know why I reached back on the ledge behind the seat for the hammer that was there. The way she looked, I knew she might carry out her threats.

"The first thing I knew I had swung the hammer. Its flat side struck her head. She screamed and started out of the car. I hit her again and again. Soon we were both out of the car. She kept cursing me, but she didn't cry for help. I struck her again with a hammer, then I struck her one real bad one. She cursed me again. I guess her last words were, 'Damn you, I'll kill you.'"

The professor said he returned home in a daze and made himself a sandwich and a glass of milk. He sat at the dining-room table, in the dark. When his wife came downstairs, she asked, "Is that you?" He affirmed that it was, and she went back to bed.

The night jailer, Tim A. Donovan, revealed that Snook had told him that while sipping milk in the dark at home, he had an urge to return to the scene and cover the body with a blanket to protect it from the rain. Donovan remembered Snook's words: "A feeling of remorse came over me when I thought about the body lying there alone on the ground and exposed to the elements." Snook did not return to the rifle range, however. Instead, he washed off the bloody hammer and pocketknife before going to bed.

"I wondered why I didn't throw the hammer away," he told reporters. "Hammers are so cheap." But then, so was Snook.

Friday the grand jury met behind doors closed to nearly 100 curiosity seekers. It heard from 28 witnesses, including Dr. Hix, who seemed adept at meeting up with the press. This time he had tears in his eyes, having just testified for 22 minutes.

"This man is getting something that is coming to him," he said of his daughter's killer, repeatedly rubbing his drawn face with his hands. "I don't believe what he says about my girl. He is the man who did all he could to break down her moral reserve. No punishment is too severe for him."

Snook relaxed in his cell at the county jail until taken in the afternoon to have his Bertillon measurements – fingerprints and photographs – taken. He engaged photographer Homer Richter in lighthearted casual conversation.

Late in the afternoon the eight women and seven men on the Franklin County Grand Jury returned a first-degree murder indictment against Snook. George A. Blood, a relative of prosecutor Chester, served as jury foreman, and George W. Lavely, father of Chester's chief investigator, Howard Lavely, sat on the jury. Arraignment was set for Monday.

The Ohio State Journal saw fit to publish in its Friday morning edition not one but two editorials commenting on the case. The first noted that "the mystery is solved and the suspense is over. The wretched murderer has confessed, endeavoring to palliate his horrible crime with a story that sounds like a plea for mercy....It would have been a dreadful thing if the perpetrator of this bloody crime had gone undetected...For years prior to the terrible climax, Dr. Snook, a supposedly respectable member of society, led a life of concealment, hypocrisy and sin. The moral lesson of his case sticks out all through the sickening story."

The second editorial noted that the case had been the "all-absorbing topic of conversation in this vicinity for the last few days. The weather and the gas rate have sunk into insignificance as subjects for discussion. Everyone, apparently, has been interested almost to the exclusion of all else in this mystery story in real life."

Truly, all Columbus talked about the case, trying to determine whether this prominent member of the OSU faculty could have done what it was said he had done. At the Woolworth 5 & 10 notions counter, at popular downtown restaurants such as The Clock and Marzetti's, at Lazarus' shoe department and certainly throughout the OSU campus, everyone had something to say about the Snook case.

In Snook's hometown of South Lebanon, *The Hamilton Daily News* reported a week after the murder that "the shock of the news... has not yet worn away, but the expression of indignant disbelief in the guilt of the veterinarian can be heard on every hand."

Police Chief Harry A. French described Snook as a "scholastic Shylock. He paid his money and extracted the flesh." The officer's comment was in reference to Snook having given Theora money to help finance her schooling.

French, the self-described "Mr. Good Guy" during the questioning of the suspect, detailed events for a *Cincinnati Post* journalist:

> Dr. Snook was convinced his intelligence was superior to that of anyone who might examine him. He laughed and sneered

through much of the questioning, trying apparently to give the impression it was a joke. When I asked him why he could keep so calm during this long grilling, while last week he was thrown into a murderous rage over a relatively unimportant argument, he did not answer.[14]

Helen Snook was anything but calm. She could not believe that her husband had been indicted for murder.

"The Howard Snook to whom I have been married seven years could not have done this thing. He always provided me with a good home. He is my husband. It is the father of my child. I will go to him as soon as I am permitted." She usually called her husband, Howard.

Was the accused sane when he took a hammer to his lover's head? Chester thought so, but to ward off an insanity plea he appointed three alienists (psychiatrists) to examine Snook on Saturday, a week after his arrest: Drs. Earl E. Gaver and Robert C. Tarbell, both associated with a private sanatorium, and Dr. William C. Pritchard, superintendent of Columbus State Hospital for the Insane.

Defense counsel gave no indication as to a course of action other than that their client would plead not guilty on Monday. "It would be foolish to reveal the nature of the defense before the trial," Seidel said.

Come Monday morning, June 24, Franklin County Common Pleas Judge Robert P. Duncan's courtroom was jammed with spectators for the arraignment, requiring a handful of uniformed deputies to maintain order. Excited by their good fortune to be in the courtroom, the crowd buzzed in anticipation. Then suddenly a hush: "Hear ye, hear ye…" intoned Bailiff Robert Thompson. Then Snook appeared.

Attired in a gray suit, red dotted tie and shoes recently polished, the veterinarian appeared composed while handcuffed to prisoner Albert C. Gunning, who was accused of shooting his wife to death in a car. Snook took his seat alongside 16 other accused criminals and calmly looked around the room. His shackled hand was still bandaged from the injury

---

[14] *The Cincinnati Post*, June 21, 1929.

he claimed he had sustained while repairing his coupe the day before the murder.

"Two weeks ago, he was a respected member among the elite of a great university," *Columbus Evening Dispatch* reporter George A. Smallsreed observed. "Now, fate had thrust him among alleged robbers, thieves and slayers."

The Court ordered Snook to stand for the reading of the indictment by Clerk of Court Joseph Palmer in Case No. 17278. As Snook rose and stood as straight as a bullet, Dr. Hix did, also, leveling a hypnotic gaze at the man who admitted to murdering his only child. It was a stare not only of deep resentment, but a look intended to further demoralize the prisoner. Hix was the person Snook least wanted to see, and Hix knew that.

"What is your plea, Dr. Snook?" Judge Duncan asked. "Guilty or not guilty?"

The reply came loud and clear, "Not guilty."

Both Seidel and Ricketts argued for a delay to allow more time to prepare the defense. Duncan denied that. They also indicated they would seek a change of venue due to the massive amount of publicity. That, too, would be denied. The trial would start Monday, July 22, Duncan said, the date of Chester's choosing. The acrimonious exchange of arguments between the defense and the prosecution was the first of many to come.

Deputy Sheriff Donovan accompanied Snook back across the Bridge of Sighs, which connected the courthouse to the county jail. Seeing so many people in the courtroom surprised his prisoner, Donovan said. "They were there to see Dr. Melvin Hix," the deputy lied.

"It's too bad, isn't it," Snook commented somewhat aimlessly.

The guard and the prisoner also spoke briefly about Gunning, who, following his arraignment, was sent to the Lima State Hospital for the Criminally Insane. "If he was judged insane," Snook said, "I don't know why I couldn't be." Chester's three alienists initially found Snook to be complex but sane, however.

Curiously, a few minutes later Donovan and Snook walked back across the Bridge of Sighs to the courtroom so photographers could get pictures of Snook posed with his attorneys, Chester and Sheriff Paul. Still more photographs with his counsel were taken once he returned to his cell.

While working the night shift in the jail, Donovan noticed that Snook had trouble sleeping. "He doesn't sleep well at all. He just seems to lie on his cot and think. He is worried about what the public thinks of him."

At one point, Snook said to no one in particular: "What's the use of living now? ... I keep seeing Theora's face all the time. If they put me away, I won't see it anymore. I don't know why it is, but I want to look again at her face, that face with the sneer she gave me the night I put her away. Even if it haunts me, I want to see it."

He never did.

7 | A VERY DIFFICULT PROBLEM

The State's intent to have jury selection begin July 22 went awry almost from the start amid legal wrangling, toothaches and shrinks. Terrorist threats did not help the situation, either.

At the outset, Franklin County Common Pleas Judge John R. Kane, who was scheduled to hear the Snook case, begged off because of a bad toothache. The duty went instead to the scholarly Judge Henry L. Scarlett, chief justice of the Franklin County Common Pleas Court. He postponed a family vacation to Glacier National Park in Montana to sit in judgment.

Both Ricketts and Max C. Seyfert of Circleville, Ohio, who had been added to the defense team, claimed medical problems. Seyfert needed "immediate" dental work, namely the extraction of teeth due to the decay in his jawbone. Ricketts, on the other hand, had been ill for some months following a paralytic stroke. His doctor told Judge Scarlett that it would be unwise for the attorney to practice during the heat of the summer, so the defense sought a continuance. Feeling the public pressure to get the trial under way, however, the judge ruled that health issues involving the defense attorneys would delay the proceedings.

Determining the defendant's sanity managed to do so, however. Chester's three psychiatrists told the Court they could not reach a conclusion on Snook's sanity without a second examination.

The defense hired its own psychiatrists, Dr. John H. Berry of the Athens (Ohio) State Hospital and Dr. G. W. Heffner of Circleville, Ohio. They examined Snook for an hour and a half, infringing on the time Chester's three doctors had planned for their follow-up evaluation.

"It is our duty to afford every possible means of defense for our client," said Seidel. "Legally we must determine whether he was mentally affected."

Chester did not make it easy for the defense, though. He insisted that Franklin County Deputy Sheriff Ephriam M. Gordon remain in the room while Berry and Heffner examined Snook. Chester's three doctors had their second chance at Snook three days later, on Monday afternoon, July 1.

On Wednesday, July 3, the defense again argued for a continuance until the fall term of the Court on the grounds that the two defense-appointed psychiatrists did not have time to complete their work.

"The time allotted for making this investigation by July 22 is utterly insufficient and might work a material injury to the accused and to the interests of justice and society at large if the examination observations and investigation were forced to be made by said date," the defense alienists maintained. To make a complete neuropsychiatric examination, they insisted on taking the time to delve into Snook's ancestry, the family's medical history, his education and his early life.

"Dr. Snook presents a very difficult problem for diagnoses, one of the most difficult I have ever seen," Dr. Berry told Judge Scarlett. "Out of 100 cases, 90 percent are easily recognized, but that is not true in this case.

"This is a case that, in our opinion, is to be of any value we must know all the facts – his early life, environment, how he has reacted to that environment."

Berry's associate, Dr. Heffner, noted that it was not until they met for the second time that Snook began to respond to questions truthfully. Initially, he said, Snook was "evasive; he was not frank with us."

Ricketts, Seidel and Seyfert argued that a July trial would be impossible to mount. They pointed to four reasons: the "rare, unusual and complex nature" of the case, the many witnesses to be examined, the extensive investigation of the law and the facts involved. Talk of a change of venue was scrapped.

Once again Judge Scarlett ruled that he could find no valid reasons for a continuance. It was now Friday, July 12, 10 days before jury selection was to begin for the biggest murder trial in the city's history. The defense had yet to receive the prosecution's evidence and list of several dozen witnesses.

"We are not satisfied with the trial date," said Ricketts. "The constitutional rights of our client are jeopardized. ...To have the trial date at that time is against the intent of the 14th Amendment."

The boisterous defense attorney also declared that he intended to attack the confession Snook gave to the prosecution, claiming it was illegal because of the many nonstop hours his client was questioned. This was but a hint of what was to come during the trial.

Every detail of the Snook case dominated the news, but every now and then another story would capture a headline or two. One featured "the world's favorite honeymooners," Charles and Anne Lindbergh, who landed a two-seat, open-cockpit aircraft at Port Columbus on Tuesday, July 2. They stayed overnight in a penthouse suite at the downtown Deschler-Wallick Hotel before continuing a celebratory barnstorming trip across the country to the West Coast.

An historic event of even greater importance took place Monday, July 8, also at Port Columbus. A host of celebrities/passengers, including the famous aviatrix Amelia Earhart, turned out for the inauguration of the nation's first transcontinental air-train service, with the westbound air portion beginning in Columbus. The airline was Transcontinental Air Transport. A year later, TAT became Trans World Airlines, or TWA.

Snook grabbed the lion's share of newsprint from his cell, much of it reporting on trivia that readers gobbled up. They were told, for instance, that the prisoner's first holiday (July Fourth) meal behind bars included pork chops, mashed potatoes, peas, beets, bread and butter and coffee. Taking a stance to demonstrate his stroke with an imaginary putter in hand, he told his jailers how much he missed his regular Saturday-morning golf game at the Scioto Country Club. And the press published an example of incredibly poor taste by Police Prosecutor L. Eugene Hensel. He informed Chester that he would step aside as a judge in a weekend bathing-beauty contest if Chester would make Snook available as a judge instead.

These and other tales continued to fascinate the press and his readers. Snook obliged by providing many of them. One who came calling was one of the nation's foremost journalists, James L. Kilgallen,[15] who worked for William Randolph Hearst's International News Service. Shortly after arriving in Columbus, he obtained an "exclusive" interview with Snook in his prison cell. Kilgallen scribbled while the professor described his plight as "a dream, a weird, unbelievable nightmare."

Snook said that he could not believe that he was involved in a murder. "I've never shown any criminal instincts. How did I come to this? I thought I was like every other normal man."

Theora was "a most desirable girl," Snook told Kilgallen, at least until she began to interfere in his life as a husband and father. "She never wanted to marry me and never asked me to divorce my wife, but when she was aroused, she was hard to deal with. She was quite an athlete."

According to Snook, Theora also had an interest in sex, having read much more on the subject than he had.

---

[15]He was the father of Dorothy Kilgallen, also a Hearst journalist/columnist, who became a popular television game-show panelist in the 1950s and early 1960s.

"I refuse the statement of her father that I broke down her moral reserve," the professor said. "That is not true. She was perfectly willing to enter into an arrangement with me."

"Any regrets?" Kilgallen asked.

"Regrets? I am overwhelmed with regrets. I am in a daze. Everything has come down upon me. I cannot tell you in words how much I do regret."

Kilgallen was just one of more than 30 journalists, representing news organizations throughout the country, expected in Columbus for the nation's largest trial. William C. Howells, a top *Plain Dealer* reporter and president of the Ohio Legislative Correspondents Association, was named chairman of the press committee to make arrangements for credentials, accommodations and telegraph facilities. It was, courthouse historians said, the first time telegraph wires would be installed in the courthouse for a trial. In addition, construction began on a press gallery of 33 seats in the courtroom, each seat assigned.

Among the journalists assigned to cover the trial was a young artist/cartoonist for *The Columbus Evening Dispatch* by the name of Milton Caniff. An Ohio State University graduate (1930), he later went on to draw the popular cartoon strips "Terry and the Pirates" and "Steve Canyon."[16]

The Ohio State Journal assigned more than a half dozen journalists to cover the trial, including Mary V. Daugherty. "She will make no attempt at sob-sistering or seeking out the so-called woman angle," the paper said. "Mrs. Daugherty can be expected to present each day a newsy story of appealing content."

Preparations for the trial went forward as well. The judge ordered that a waist-high metal railing be erected to hold back the anticipated 150 seated and standing spectators. The jury would be seated facing the bench, their backs to the spectators immediately behind them. In addition, five additional bailiffs, earning $6.25 each per day, were

---

[16] Other artists working in pen and ink were Dudley Fisher, a syndicated artist for King Features Syndicate, and Ted Keys of *The Columbus Evening Dispatch*.

assigned to the Court to maintain order. Spectators closest to the doors at 8 a.m. and 1 p.m. on trial days would be entitled to enter the courtroom until it reached capacity.

Columbus police had just about given up hope of having an eyewitness to the murder when Clarence R. Murray came forward. The evening of the murder, he drove past the New York Central Railroad rifle range on his way home from his brother's house, he told detectives McCall and Phillips. It was dusk, about 8 p.m. Sitting in the backseat of his Maxwell were his daughters Flossie, 11, and Bertha, 13; he and the "missus" had 10 children in all and another was on the way.

Murray, a carpenter by trade, said he saw a woman with long brown hair and a man standing beside a blue Ford coupe, apparently arguing. "It seemed like they were scuffling." The woman had her hands on the man's chest as though she was pushing him away, Murray recalled, but he could not see their faces. As he got a little closer, the couple separated, one going to one side of the car and the other to the opposite side.

Why hadn't he reported what he had seen sooner? He said he was afraid of the publicity that would result. Also, his wife was pregnant and ill. She didn't want him to say anything at all. In any event, he hardly was the "eyewitness" the prosecution had hoped for.

Investigators became excited over more news, only to have their bubble burst again. Initially it was thought that a 17-year-old, Lawrence Kuhn, had found Theora's purse, which Snook claimed he had thrown into the Scioto River. The purse was not Theora's, however. The victim's purse never surfaced.

In a surprise move Monday morning (July 15), Ricketts announced that his client would plead insanity at the time of the murder, raising the possibility of a delay of several days in the proceedings. It also opened a legal can of worms, forcing the court, the prosecution and the defense to make contingency plans. For example, Judge Scarlett would have to call a separate jury panel of 12 for the sanity trial. Nine jurors would have to agree to a verdict.

The insanity case would have to be heard first – beginning July 22. Several complex courses were then possible: Snook might end up in the Lima State Hospital for the Criminally Insane; he could be set free if found sane but did not know right from wrong at the time of the killing, or he could be determined sane and be put on trial for first-degree murder.

In preparation for the insanity defense, the Court appointed its own psychiatrists. (A total of eight were now on the Snook case.) Dr. W. H. Vorbau, superintendent of the Lima State Hospital for the Criminally Insane; Dr. Guy H. Williams, superintendent of the Cleveland State Hospital, and Dr. Arthur G. Hyde, superintendent of the Massillon (Ohio) State Hospital, represented the State. At Judge Scarlett's direction, they first conferred with the five alienists for the defense and the prosecution and then met with Snook the afternoon of Thursday, July 18. They concluded their examination in less than an hour and a half, giving rise to speculation that they had found Snook to be sane. Judge Scarlett said he would read their individually prepared reports on Saturday.

By then, however, the defense team had changed its plans once again, announcing that it would not seek an insanity defense. It also waived the sanity hearing. When asked if that meant Snook would plead guilty, Ricketts replied: "No, emphatically no! We will go to trial under the indictment Wednesday morning."

The switch, courthouse mavens said, would allow the defense team to go for a verdict of not guilty by virtue of insanity rather than run the risk of having Snook found sane at a sanity hearing and thus eliminate the insanity issue altogether. Also, the Snook team did not want the court's psychiatrists to present their findings, given the implications in the speed of their examination.

Ricketts drew another fine line. He maintained that Snook may have been "medically sane…but legally insane" when he bludgeoned Theora to death. The attorney promised to make the trial "a simple one, not in the least complicated."

The defense also attacked their client's confession. Seidel told the press Monday, "We have in our possession the facts of the real motive of the crime, and the State's alleged confession is not worth the paper it is written on." He claimed his client was "not in his proper frame of mind."

Dr. and Mrs. Hix continued to receive press attention as they waited for the trial to begin. The newspapers noted that while in Columbus, they had received a number of letters from their daughter's friends and schoolmates. "I know your hearts are broken and mine aches with you and for you," wrote Ella L. Vinal, who attended the seminary with Theora. "I loved Theora so much. I can't understand how anyone would harm her."

Somebody seemed intent on harming Ricketts' 19-year-old daughter, Helen. Her mother, Minnie, said she had received two "terrorist" telephone calls from a man and a woman, both threatening Helen with kidnapping and bodily harm if her father continued to represent Snook.

"They said Mr. Ricketts would have to get out of the case by Monday at the latest," Mrs. Ricketts said. "I could tell from their voices they were not of the roughneck type. They had fine, cultured voices. Of course Mr. Ricketts will not keep out of the case," adding that he had asked for and received police protection for his daughter.

"These threats strike at a spot where it is most tender," said Mrs. Ricketts. "I'm not leaving Helen out of my sight at any time."

Ricketts' associate in the case, Seidel, revealed that he had received a couple of anonymous threats, also. One came in a postcard ordering him out of the case. The writer said that Seidel would be "doomed" if he didn't walk away from the defense. Another note threatened to tar and feather all three defense attorneys if they did not abandon the Snook case.

Later Assistant County Prosecutor Paul Hicks received a crank letter. The writer threatened to kidnap his wife if he continued to "persecute" the defendant. The author asked for $1,000, adding: "If you cannot get the new currency, bring a full bushel of afrodizzyak" (sic).

Despite such disturbing developments, the eagerly awaited capital murder trial apparently would begin at last with jury selection at 9 a.m. Wednesday, July 24. A venire of 75 citizens, including 16 women, was called for jury duty.

8 | GETTING A JURY

Although Judge Scarlett's courtroom on the third floor was the largest in the 42-year-old Franklin County Courthouse, it would be taxed to its capacity during the trial of the horse doctor. The first of 500 would-be spectators lined up at the courthouse doors at 4:45 a.m. Wednesday – Ohio State University dental student Edgar Williams and his wife, Ruby,[17] led the way – hoping for a courtroom seat. It would be more than three hours before the court's doors opened for the first day of jury selection.

Once they did, pushing and shoving was the order of the day, making it necessary for Sheriff Harry Paul to threaten jail time for anyone who pushed. "Ladies and gentlemen, the spectators' gallery is filled and the only way you can get in now is when someone leaves," he said. The crowd stood fast and was rewarded when Paul permitted 51 more to enter as standees. Among those who made it was 17-year-old Ted Cramer. He had hitchhiked to Columbus from his home in Peoria, Illinois, just to attend the trial.[18]

---

[17] One newspaper reported that Bernard Gatrell and his sister, Betty, were first in line.
[18] Lillian Nolish and her friend, Martha Feldman, of Cleveland also hitchhiked to Columbus for the trial.

Young women "of the flapper-type" made up more than half of the gallery. Others with time on their hands during the day were, *The Columbus Evening Dispatch* observed, "veterans of the old red-light district."

Mr. and Mrs. Williams, Cramer and their fellow spectators in the courtroom waited another hour before being electrified by the arrival of the principal players in the deadly drama. At one tick of the clock past 9 a.m., Bailiff Carl F. Beck ordered everyone to stand while Judge Scarlett ascended to the bench. Immediately thereafter a buzz went through the room. "There he is!" "That's him!" "That's Dr. Snook!" Scarlett gaveled for order as Sheriff Paul led the accused to his seat at the defense table between Ricketts and Seidel. Attired in the gray suit he wore when arrested, a white shirt, starched collar and a spotted red tie, the defendant could have been mistaken for an attorney on the defense team. A clean bandage protected his wounded right hand.

Arriving a few minutes earlier was the prosecution's team, led by Chester and assistant prosecutors Myron B. Gessaman and Paul C. Hicks. With his fine features, blue eyes and slicked black hair, Chester cut a suave figure for the ladies in attendance. He wasn't known as "Handsome Jack" for nothing.

Flexing his fingers to ready for his task ahead was Roscoe R. Walcutt, the first of three stenographers from the firm of Armstrong & Okey assigned to the trial: Howard B. Diltz and Eldon B. Rowe were the other two. Working in 30-minute shifts, they took down testimony in shorthand jottings that a staff of seven then typed and assembled for the daily transcript.

Judge Scarlett told the prospective jurors what they could expect. "This case has received a great deal of publicity, and there may be some difficulty in getting a jury. It must be tried solely on the testimony of sworn witnesses and without bias or prejudice. You cannot be accepted as a juror unless you can lay aside any pre-conceived impressions of this case." In particular, the judge noted the statewide interest in the case "because of the large number of Ohio State University alumni who feel the university connections." Finally, he warned against any discussion of the case.

The rather portly Miss Edith Dysinger, a retired nurse who once worked in a hospital psychiatric ward, was the first potential juror called for questioning by the confident Chester.

"Have you any objections to the death penalty in a proper case where the facts warrant?" he began.

"No, sir," she replied.

"None whatsoever?"

"No, sir."

She went on to say in response to a question from the judge that she thought she could "lay aside all prejudices."

Defense attorney Seidel asked her if she had any prejudices "against the defendant pleading insanity at the time of the commission of the crime." She said she didn't.

The death penalty and insanity were two subjects that came up repeatedly during the questioning of the likely jurors. Another was drugs.

During the routine questioning of Miss Dysinger, Seidel suddenly pointed his finger at her: "Do you know what aphrodisiacs are?" When she said she didn't, he explained that they were drugs designed to "stimulate sexual excitement in human beings."

The question opened up the subject of drugs. For several weeks there had been speculation that either Snook or Theora, or both, used drugs to stimulate their passion. As the press said, it was "the dope angle" of the case. Drugs and "illicit sexual relations" would be brought up during the trial, Seidel promised the prospective jurors. His client was an unwilling victim, of course, a mere sex slave.

Snook maintained that neither he nor Theora were drug users, but as the case unfolded, narcotics kept playing a role. Assistant U.S. District Attorney William B. Bartles' earlier investigation determined that drugs had had no connection with the murder. He was anxious, however, to continue the probe of the larger issue, that of the availability of drugs at the university.

"Morphine and cocaine were kept in an unlocked desk drawer from which it could be taken by almost anyone," Bartles discovered. "I can imagine nothing more dangerous. I propose to take the matter up with President Rightmire and with the state attorney general, if necessary, to find out why such conditions are permitted to exist."

The defense thought it had a much better chance with an all-male jury than one sprinkled with women. As the questioning proceeded, it appeared that a number of women had made up their mind as to Snook's guilt or innocence. Consequently, they were excused.

Dysinger was not, however. She was the first to be temporarily seated in the jury box, but later she would be dismissed under unusual circumstances.

Despite wide-open windows and the valiant effort of one electric fan, courtroom attendees sweltered under temperatures that topped 90 degrees in the afternoon – except for Snook, who seemed cool and calm throughout the six-hour session. For much of the day he slouched in his chair, scribbling notes on a pad, seemingly uninterested in the proceedings. When Judge Scarlett invited the men in the courtroom to remove their jackets, Snook continued to wear his, as did the attorneys. An extra water cooler was placed near the defense table.

Anticipating a crush of courthouse visitors, the first-floor refreshment stand ordered extra ice and soft drinks. The stand did a brisk lunchtime business. Courthouse janitor Vic T. Stanton admired the newspaper photograph of him passing out to perspiring spectators cracked ice from a bucket.

Seidel's questioning of Mrs. Nellie E. McClintock, wife of a wholesale grocery salesman, brought a gasp from the courtroom crowd. He asked her: "Could you, in the mixed company of your fellow jurors, thoroughly and fully discuss Miss Hix's and Dr. Snook's relations without embarrassment, even if such discussion led into the subject of unnatural sex relations?" It was a question that he would ask again and again, much to the distress of the victim's parents.

"I could," the blushing mother of three replied.

There were fewer than half the number of spectators waiting to gain entrance to the courtroom on Thursday as there had been Wednesday. In fact, during the morning session there were quite a few empty seats. The jury selection continued its measured pace with questions about drugs, insanity, capital punishment and the possibility of "filthy testimony." Snook, looking relaxed, continued to take notes on a pad. As if to mock the defendant's actions, Dr. Hix also had a pad for notes. Flanking him was his attorney, Boyd B. Haddox, and Mrs. Hix, who fanned herself vigorously with an old-fashion palmetto-leaf fan that suited her. Each time a prospective juror voiced an objection to capital punishment, she lifted her eyeglasses and dabbed her tears with a linen handkerchief. She, for one, obviously wanted her daughter's killer to fry in the electric chair.

By the end of the day, however, the elderly couple had left the courtroom. After conferring with Haddox by telephone, Dr. Hix's Florida physician, Dr. John M. Thomas, determined that the trial would put too much strain on Hix's weak heart.

Apparently Seidel's promise of "filthy testimony" drew a large, rambunctious crowd to the courthouse Friday, perhaps the largest yet. Folks buzzed with excitement and giggled at what they found funny. Several times Special Bailiff James McShane had to call the gallery to order. It was hot once again, forcing the Court to turn off the large lights over the spectators seating. The jury selection process seemed as interminable as the heat. Nothing filthy surfaced. When the Court adjourned for the weekend, all the participants knew more of the same drudgery would face them Monday morning and continue until a panel was selected.

"The state is satisfied with the jury as now constituted," Chester said late Friday, but the defense intended to continue to exercise its challenges, hoping to keep as many women as possible off the panel. Females were likely to shy away from intense discussion of unnatural sexual activity, the defense believed.

Friday night Helen Snook and her mother-in-law visited Snook at the jail for about 20 minutes. Mary E. Snook, 73, tried to keep on a happy face for her son. "Look, Jimmy, how do you like my new dress?" she asked.

Only after she had left the jail did she reveal the depth of her distress. "I wouldn't let Jimmy see how brokenhearted I am. I just put my arms around him and loved him and asked him how he felt. I wouldn't cry then," she said, but afterward she did.

Her tears flowed freely as she recalled the Saturday he was arrested. He and his family were expected at a family reunion in Lebanon. He said he would telephone her when he left Columbus, "but the call never came," she said. Neither did he.

Helen Snook made a brief visit to her husband Saturday to bring him clean clothes. This time she arrived alone.

She had been in virtual seclusion for most of July, avoiding the early days of the trial, but she gave an exclusive interview to Anne Schatenstein of *The Columbus Evening Dispatch* on Thursday, July 25. The distraught wife told of her happiness with her husband and her loyalty to him.

"He loved to be with me," she said. "We went out often together. He enjoyed taking me around with him to meet his friends, his business and professional associates and the persons whom he knew through his hobby of pistol shooting. We were happy, really happy, I tell you.

"But things changed within the last three years. I lost him, little by little, more and more. It was gradually, just gradually. I knew not how or why. I did not question."

Not only had he been a devoted husband, Helen said, "but he was the kindest and most considerate son to his parents I have ever witnessed in my experience."

Asked if she wanted a divorce, Helen replied, "No, never have I wanted a divorce from him. I do not want a divorce now," she said softly, almost inaudibly.

When Court opened Monday morning, 11 jurors had been tentatively seated, three of them women. Nevertheless, the judge had ordered 50 more prospects to the courthouse inasmuch as the original group of 75 had dwindled to a few. Later he would summon another venire of 30.

A chipper Chester told the press what he thought of the trial's progress. He was convinced that the defense would have to put the accused on the stand. "He is the main witness in support of its contentions that he was insane and that he acted in self-defense," Chester said. "I have witnesses whom I have not yet named to support my contentions that the results of using aphrodisiacs are not the same as explained by the defense while he was cross-examining prospective jurors.

"This story about 'love potions' is all the bunk," he concluded.

On Monday, July 29, newspapers reported that Snook was "near collapse." Accompanied by a nurse, Columbus pathologist Dr. Howard N. Brundage had administered a spinal tap in jail Saturday morning in order to rule out anything unusual – specifically syphilis – that could be indicative of a brain disorder and point to Snook's unusual behavior.

"The fluid which Dr. Brundage removed evidently affected my entire nervous system," Snook said. "If I get up suddenly from a reclining position, everything seems blank." Then he added: "The next one who tries punching my spine will get a punch in the nose."

The Court denied a defense plea for abandonment of the Monday afternoon session because of Snook's malady, which had taken its toll on the defendant. He seemed irritable during the afternoon session, glaring impatiently at the whispering people behind him. A couple of gentlemen in the gallery were admonished by bailiffs for snoring.

The Court initially denied a cot for Snook, but Dr. Brundage examined the veterinarian once again and recommended that the defendant be given some measure of comfort. On Tuesday, Judge Scarlett ordered a low-slung Deauville beach chair be delivered to the courtroom. The chair's canvas blared bright orange, interrupted by stripes of yellow, green, black and brown. According to one reporter, it was "by far the gaudiest piece of furniture the stodgy old courtroom has ever seen."

Snook was not given newspapers to read, but had he been able to do so, he would have read in Monday's *Columbus Citizen* that he was "really a gifted man, clever, original, inventive, practical…mentally alert, good-natured, affable [and] very sensitive emotionally."

This was the evaluation of Cedric W. Lemont, a local astrologer, who prepared an extensive horoscope for Snook. Lemont went on to the say, "In spite of the splendid natural mental abilities and of the really pleasing and attractive disposition pictured here, Dr. Snook's chart is a very unfortunate one in many ways. It shows a decided trend toward litigation and trouble through the law."

As for Theora's horoscope, Lemont said that he had "never seen more fatalistic conditions that existed in [her] chart on the evening of June 13 when she came to her death. The progressed moon was in opposition to Uranus, with Saturn and the sun transiting adversely to both and to the progressed Venus as well."

Apparently the planets did not look favorably on the jury selection. Wednesday morning, just as it appeared that the panel was in place, it suffered a loss. While standing at the lunch counter having a sandwich and soda on Tuesday, Miss Dysinger engaged in casual conversation with defense attorney Max Seyfert. He knew her family in Amanda, Ohio, and recalled that 40 years earlier his father had bought a racehorse from her uncle, John Dysinger. The attorney told her that as a result his father had named the horse "Johnny D."

"The conversation didn't amount to anything," she said, "and it never entered my head that I shouldn't be talking to him."

Joe Costa, a photographer for the *New York Daily News*, captured the chance meeting. When the photograph and the conversation came to the attention of Judge Scarlett, all sides agreed it would be best if Miss Dysinger be excused.

"I wasn't particularly interested in this case, and now that I have heard so many of the questions about what the testimony will be about, I am just as well pleased to be excused," she said. "I think it is going to be pretty dirty."

Finally, after nearly six days of questioning 107 citizens, a jury of 11 men and one woman, plus an alternate, was seated Wednesday morning, July 31. Mrs. Helen E. Lunsford, a housewife, was the only woman on the panel.

Wednesday afternoon the jurors piled into four sedans and, with press and officials trailing, took an organized tour of places key to the murder investigation: the love nest; the residences of the victim and the accused, the university and its veterinary clinic where Snook had his office, the Scioto Country Club, the New York Central Railroad rifle range, etc. The 23-mile round-trip was quiet and uneventful, save for an outburst from a bystander at the range. "Hang the old devil! He ought to be hung!" he yelled at the jurors as they walked the killing field, now thoroughly trampled by curiosity seekers.

Completely oblivious to the juror's tour, Snook exhibited a jovial mood. "I have had more rest this summer than any for several years," he told a jailer. "I don't have to worry about any duties." He also revealed that he had gained four pounds while imprisoned and his severe headaches were now "nice and ordinary."

After the panel had completed its tour, it was sequestered at the fashionable Southern Hotel on S. High Street for the duration of the trial. All seemed in readiness for opening statements Thursday, but about 4 a.m., Mrs. Lunsford, 40, suffered a "hemorrhage" in her lungs and arrived in court, frail and feeling poorly. After conferring with both the prosecution and the defense, Judge Scarlett excused her. Mrs. Harry (Betty) Cassady, the alternate who thought she would be able to return to her canning in a couple of days, replaced Mrs. Lunsford, and Newton L. Tracy, a Pennsylvania Railroad foreman, became the alternate. He was given a hasty tour in the morning to catch up with what the remainder of the panel had observed the previous day.

In addition to Mrs. Cassady and Tracy, the jury consisted of Jacob C. Rehl, a public accountant; Frank H. Joyce, a blacksmith; Charles F. Butche, a carpenter; Charles S. Baird, who would become foreman, Raymond Hann, and Clyde Moody, all three farmers; Wilby L. Balthaser, a grocer; Paul L. Weaver, a wholesale coal dealer; Edward

W. Hoe, a salesman; Harold E. Brown, a shoe worker; and Roy C. Stiffey, an engineer for the Ohio Inspection Bureau.

A light rain fell on Columbus Thursday afternoon, cooling off the city's heat wave. Everyone now expected the heat to come from trial testimony.

9 | THE DIRECT CAUSE OF DEATH

The defendant "did unlawfully, purposely, and of deliberate and premeditated malice make an assault...to kill and murder..."

As Chester opened his argument with a reading of the murder indictment, Snook reclined in his beach chair and stared at the ceiling. He seemed oblivious to the prosecutor's account of the night Theora Hix died, the manner in which she died and what steps the accused took to cover up his crime.

The record gallery hung on every word. Several hundred had lined up early Thursday morning (August 1), only to realize they had to wait until the afternoon session for testimony to begin. Among them once again was 65-year-old Edward Clark, who had not missed a moment of the proceedings. However, he and the other spectators could see very little of the main attraction: Snook. Just the top of his virtually bald head was visible as he slouched down in his beach chair.

Chester launched into a reading of the coroner's autopsy, describing the wounds one by one, and holding up to the jury the "murder implements" and articles of Theora's clothing. When he showed the jury her garter belt, Seidel piped up.

"If the Court please, I don't want to disturb Mr. Chester, but it seems to me that that is almost like testifying, and I might make the objection exhibiting all the exhibits before they are identified." Judge Scarlett agreed.

"They are going to be placed in evidence," Chester said. In starting anew, he again held up the undergarments.

Seidel again interrupted: "I don't want to be pestiferous, but really that is direct testimony on a matter that could not be established. I make an objection."

Chester continued unabated. Ricketts joined in the fray, objecting to "this alleged exhibit." Chester went on, ignoring the defense. It was the first of many battles, the next one coming within minutes, when Chester referred to a newspaper report that a sandwich had been found in Theora's stomach.

"We are not trying the newspapers," Ricketts said, "and I do not think it is competent here to show anything that the newspapers may have said. We are already saturated now with newspaper stuff in this case."

"Well, we will help you saturate it," Chester said smugly, continuing with his statement once again.

"Wait a minute!" a red-faced Ricketts roared. "I object to this case being argued here. That is purely an argument. It isn't anything else but an argument, and a self-serving declaration on the part of the State's counsel."

Judge Scarlett overruled the objection. Moments later he did so again when Chester held up a bottle of Spanish fly[19] that he said was found in Snook's campus office. Finally, after about 40 minutes, Chester completed his presentation to the jury. Now it was the defense's turn, and "Roaring" Ricketts dropped a bombshell called "involuntary confessions."

Chester jumped to his feet and objected, noting that he had never mentioned confessions in his statement.

---

[19] Spanish fly is a blister beetle known in pharmacology as L*ytta vesicatoria* or *Cantharis vesicatoria*. Long recognized as an aphrodisiac, it's sometimes given to livestock to heighten the sex drive.

"I know you have not. I know you have concealed it, but we are going to open it up now," the defense attorney said, stammering in his excitement and glaring at the prosecutor. Ricketts was livid – "on the verge of a stroke," one reporter wrote. Judge Scarlett hammered for order when he heard laughter in the gallery.

The Court allowed Ricketts to read the applicable law concerning confessions, to wit: "Involuntary confessions are not admissible in evidence. A confession is involuntary if obtained through fear, threats, hope of reward, personal abuse or violence, direct or applied promise by authorities, artifice, playing on emotions, invective statements, over persuasion, coercion, ill-usage, assault, persistent questioning and fright, intimidation or undue influence or duress."

Ricketts wanted the Court to rule out "involuntary confessions." He said that his client was subjected to 23 hours of questioning and assaulted by Chester, "who was sworn to uphold the law – an actual assault [was] committed by him...upon the face of the defendant." It was the first time the assault on Snook had come to light. Judge Scarlett put the issue on the shelf, suggesting it be taken up again when the prosecution introduced the confession, which Chester said he would do.

When the legal sparring came to a temporary halt, Ricketts continued with his opening statement. Eventually, he said, the jury would be able to see that when Snook "committed this crime, he was absolutely insane, that Theora Hix was insane, and that this man Meyers was insane. There were three of them that were insane." Ricketts took fewer than 15 minutes to state the case for the defense, namely "self-defense and an impaired mentality on the part of the defendant."

Theora's roommate, Alice Bustin, took the stand as the prosecution's first witness. She was asked to identify the garments Theora wore the night of the killing. Assistant Prosecutor Hicks held up each item as a State's exhibit, then questioned the witness about Theora's personal habits, whether she would take any drugs or read any pornographic books.

"We had no books of that kind, and she couldn't have had any without my knowing it," the witness said.

Bustin denied anything improper but admitted her roommate did not take her into her confidence. For example, Bustin admitted she knew that Theora kept a small pistol in her dresser, but they never discussed it.

Her testimony was forthright but revealed little of substance. The same could be said for the next witness, Bertha Dillon, the telephone operator at University Hospital with whom Theora had an appointment the night of the murder. She confirmed that she spent about an hour with Theora on switchboard procedures: That was about it. The pleasing 21-year-old was eager to get off the witness stand because her fiancé was waiting for her at the church. Two hours after testifying, she became Mrs. Norman Dungan.

On his way back to his cell after Thursday's session, Snook complained about Chester's treatment in his opening statement. "He isn't giving me a square deal," the veterinarian said. "He is charging some things he cannot prove."

FRIDAY, AUGUST 2

Before the second day of the trial began, two women had fainted from the heat and lack of fresh air in the hallway. One decided to go home, the second recovered and made it into the courtroom gallery. Although smoking was forbidden in the courtroom, a young man lit a cigarette. A bailiff escorted him out.

The first prosecution witness of the day was Clarence R. Murray, who drove past the rifle range the night of the murder and observed a couple "scuffling around...The man had his arm around the lady's waist, and she had her hands up against his breast." At the prosecution's request, Murray left the witness stand to illustrate for the jury the "scuffling" he saw. He posed as the woman; Assistant Prosecutor Gessaman posed as the man, wrapping his arms around Murray while the witness placed his palms on the attorney's shoulders.

"Could you identify these people?" Seidel asked on cross-examination.

"I could not."

"You don't know who they were?"

"No, sir."

Murray said as he drove past, "I thought maybe she wanted help or something, the way they were scuffling, and if she did, she would holler. So I didn't give it a second thought then."

"You didn't give it a second thought?" Seidel asked.

"When she didn't say anything."

"And you didn't get your second thought until two or three weeks after that?"

"Oh, yes, I got my second thought, but I mean about helping her."

Inasmuch as the witness failed to identify either individual as Snook or Theora, Ricketts sought to have Murray's testimony stricken, but the Court overruled the motion.

Paul Krumlauf, one of the two teens who discovered the victim's body at the range, and Ephraim Johnson, the farmer who was plowing a nearby field, testified as to their actions the day of the discovery. Columbus Police Corporal John B. May did likewise. Some in the gallery were falling asleep. Snook's beach chair was the only bright spot.

It took the testimony of Franklin County Coroner Dr. Joseph A. Murphy to perk things up in the stuffy courtroom. Under Chester's guidance, he recalled his examination of the body at the scene and then at the morgue. He was asked to identify State's exhibit No. 1, the belted bloodstained brown silk dress with a wide ecru collar that Theora wore. Chester paraded it in front of the jury, purposely stopping right in front of the jovial Mrs. Cassady, a tailor. As he knew she would, she paid particular attention when Chester pointed out how the shoulder of the dress had been slashed, as he knew she would. Snook turned his head away, but a few in the gallery stood up to get a better look at the garment. A bailiff called for order.

Murphy ordered the body embalmed before the autopsy, which he performed Saturday morning while police were knocking on Snook's door to take him in for questioning. One by one the coroner identified the injuries "made with a round, pointed instrument… the large end of a hammer." There were "probably 12 or 13" wounds on her head, he said, and fragments of the skull were found to have pierced her brain. For the edification of the jury – and a little bit of added drama – Chester provided his head so that the doctor could point out the location of the wounds.

On the left side of Theora's neck, Murphy said, was a cut 4 ½ inches long that severed the jugular vein and "almost" cut in two a carotid artery.

"As a result of your examination, doctor, will you please give this jury the direct cause, the primary cause, of the death of Theora K. Hix."

"I am not finished with my post-mortem yet," said the physician, who continued. In reality, he had little to add except to say the victim was not pregnant. Finally, he reached a conclusion:

"I found that she had come to her death from the hemorrhage from the severing of the muscles in the neck."

"Caused by the knife wound to the neck?"

"Yes, sir."

"And the secondary cause of death, doctor?"

"Was hemorrhage – the knife wound."

Seidel initiated the cross-examination for the defense with obscure medical questions concerning "the fissure of Rolando," "the pons Varolii" and "the medullo oblongato" – all terms related to the brain and its functions. Dr. Murphy admitted that he had "not paid much attention to [these particulars] for about 40 years.... We have specialists at every division of medicine to look after those special things."

Using a large, riotously colored illustration of the human torso, Seidel questioned the coroner about every blow to the head and every knife wound in such detail that even the doctor had trouble following. The blows, the coroner admitted, "would knock a person off their feet – knock them senseless."

"Absolutely senseless?" Seidel asked.

"Yes, absolutely senseless."

"Would they be sufficient to kill?"

Murphy agreed that they would if the victim did not receive medical attention.

The defense got what it wanted: an admission that Theora's death *could* have been due to a hemorrhage caused by the hammer blows. This brought into question the indictment, which stated the knife wounds were the cause of death.

Seidel made every effort to paint Murphy's work as sloppy, because the coroner did not know certain procedures or he ignored certain tests, such as an X-ray to determine if the neck was broken. He also was asked if the victim's urine had been checked for cocaine or other drugs.

"No."

"What is the only test that can be made to determine whether or not the patient, when he died, or the party, when he died, was under the influence of cocaine?"

"I would not know how to answer that question. I never had any experience with it."

Charles C. Clay, an embalmer who worked on the victim's corpse at the mortuary, took the witness stand next. Hicks asked him how much blood came from her body in the embalming process. About a pint, he replied.

"And how many pints of blood is [sic] there in the ordinary body?"

"Well, sir, in the ordinary body there is between a gallon and a gallon than a half of blood." Due to her hemorrhaging, most of Theora's blood drained into the weeds at the rifle range.

Mrs. Freda Bowen followed Clay as a witness. She was on duty at the Brown Dye House the day after the murder, when Snook brought garments in to be cleaned, including the suit he wore the night before. When she read that he had been arrested, she examined the suit more carefully, finding stains on a sleeve. In his testimony, her associate, Newton Fisher, discovered similar stains.

"There were two blood spots on the right leg," he said. The defense immediately objected.

"Now wait!" Ricketts shouted.

"You wait!" Assistant Prosecutor Gessaman responded. "I am getting tired of being interrupted."

The angry defense attorney hurled back: "I don't care how tired you're getting!" Once again it took the Court to calm things down.

SATURDAY, AUGUST 3

Such was the continued interest in the trial that spectators hoping for a seat at Saturday's session began lining up at 11:30 p.m. Friday. Courthouse custodians allowed the early arrivals into the building to escape the nighttime rain. It was hot and humid, but some had brought blankets to nap on the floor of the third-floor corridor until the first of the spectators were admitted to the courtroom.

Columbus Police Detective Larry F. Van Skaik was called by Assistant Prosecutor Gessaman as the first witness Saturday. The officer recalled the Saturday in June he went to Snook's home to take the professor downtown for questioning. He helped Snook tie his necktie – Snook's hand was bandaged at the time – and helped him on with his jacket. Together they went to police headquarters, stopping along the way for breakfast.

Gessaman turned the questioning to Van Skaik's search for clues on the rifle range. "What, if anything, did you find?"

"We found ... a broken keychain with three keys on it, and scattered around on the ground ... we found 12 keys and the broken key ring." The 38-year-old detective's testimony was finished.

Assistant Prosecutor Hicks next called Mrs. Smalley, who recalled renting the love nest to "Mr. and Mrs." Snook in February. The arrangement was that she would clean the room on Saturdays only; "Mrs. Snook" would clean the room during the week. Also, the couple would provide their own towels: "They were extra fine Turkish towels," she said, not at all like the worn thrift shop finds she provided renters.

The prosecution's questions primarily focused on the days after the killing. The next day, June 14, Snook visited the love nest for the last time, telling the landlady he was leaving for Washington Court House – about 40 miles away. He added that his wife would not give up the room until Sunday, she recalled. Mrs. Smalley visited his room on Saturday and retrieved from the dresser the two room keys she originally had given to Snook. In the closet she found a woman's brown felt hat, one that Snook had bought for Theora. Only later that day did Mrs. Smalley see the evening paper and a photograph of Snook on the front page.

On cross-examination by Seyfert, Mrs. Smalley got a laugh from the gallery. The attorney asked if the "salt salesman" – Dr. Snook – had any satchels or valises with him when he leased the room.

"He did not have any with him."

"Did he make any effort to try to make any sale of any kind to you?"

"He did not. I don't need any salt."

The prosecution called next Dr. Oscar V. Brumley, professor of veterinary surgery at Ohio State University. He and Snook had known each other for more than 20 years. Gessaman handed the professor a bottle and asked him to identify it.

"Those are what are commonly called Spanish flies."

"Any other name for them?"

"*Cantharis vesicatoria* is the name." Brumley said the bottle had been found in Snook's office. Probably it was a classroom sample that had been around the college for quite some time, he said.

On cross-examination, Seidel wanted to know about Brumley's contacts with Theora. "Did you ever have any conversation with her concerning Dr. Snook?" he asked.

"I think I just cautioned her about going out with anyone around the department in the machine [automobile]."

Seidel returned to the Spanish fly, wanting to know if that was an aphrodisiac... a sexual stimulant. The professor explained that in animals it produces a sedative action; he could not say the effect on a human.

When the Snook case broke, Brumley was acting dean of the College of Veterinary Medicine in the absence of Dean David S. White, who had been in California and Colorado for two months, only returning the night before the opening of the trial. White then spoke publicly about the case for the first time. He told a *Columbus Citizen* reporter that "months ago" he had heard that Snook was a "woman chaser."

"I dismissed it as idle gossip and thought no more of it," he said. It was to cost him his position with the university.

Analytical chemist Charles F. Long, the last prosecution witness before the weekend recess, testified that he found "human blood" on articles of Snook's clothing, on the ex-professor's automobile and on the ball-peen hammer found in his home. Long also matched hair found in the coupe with Theora's and discovered undigested beef in her stomach as well as "four cucumber seeds, a small piece of paper, [and] some strawberry seeds." He estimated the contents had been in her stomach less than an hour before she died. He also discovered traces of a stimulant and an aphrodisiac in powdered form: *Cannabis indica* (marijuana), and cantharides, or blister beetle (Spanish fly).

The paper found in Theora's stomach, Long said on cross-examination, "was the exact type of paper" that came from a manila paper bag used for sandwiches by a filling station-convenience store at the corner of Cambridge Boulevard and the River Road, just on the southwestern edge of the Scioto Country Club property. Had Theora picked up a sandwich while riding around in the taxi, or did she and Snook stop there on their way to the rifle range? And why would she have paper from a sack in her stomach? No explanation ever came forth in the trial.

The Court adjourned the Saturday session until Monday morning. Chester expected to complete the prosecution's case Monday afternoon or Tuesday, he said. Ricketts told the press that he would call Helen Snook to testify in defense of her husband.

Unexpectedly Saturday night, Judge Scarlett faced having to declare a mistrial. After dinner, Mrs. Cassady, the lone juror of her gender, asked to visit the Franklin County jail because her husband's father had a hand in building it. The matron assigned to her, Mrs. Mayme Weir, and Mrs. Cassady walked from the Southern Hotel to the jail – where Snook was held – but the juror spoke to no one while there. After reviewing the facts surrounding the incident, Judge Scarlett chose not to remove Mrs. Cassady from the panel.

SUNDAY, AUGUST 4

Bailiffs escorted jurors either to St. John's Evangelical Lutheran Church on Mound Street or St. Joseph's Cathedral on Broad Street for Sunday services. In the afternoon they attended a baseball game at Neil Park where they observed the Rochester Clothiers, a Columbus team, defeat the Toledo Travelers.

As for Snook, he sat for an hour on a wooden bench at the jail, listening to a sermon by the Rev. C. E. Parks, who spoke under the auspices of the Columbus Prison Association. After Sunday dinner Snook commented favorably on the menu: roast pork, gravy, applesauce, and "some kind of pie; I can't remember what."

Each evening Snook wrote notes on a pad while alone in his cell to help him remember details of his case. Some thought he was writing an autobiography, but actually they were little more than thoughts, some of which he passed to his counsel the next day. The remainder he tore up into small pieces and disposed of them in the wastepaper basket.

10 | JOURNALISTS TAKE THE STAND

In the wee hours of Monday morning, the curious began to line up outside the Mound Street entrance to the courthouse. By the time the sun came up, more than 150 were in line, including Mr. and Mrs. E. R. Rule of Jacksonville, Florida. They were on a driving tour of Ohio that included a stop in Columbus to "go snooking," a phrase that came into common usage during the trial in Ohio's capital city.

As the crowd became more eager to reach the third floor, pushing and shoving ensued. Two matronly women, who said they had arrived at 3:30 a.m. Monday, fainted while standing in line, overcome by human aromas laced with the tobacco smoke that thickened the air in the 8-foot-wide hallway. They were taken to Judge Scarlett's chambers to recover. When they did, they were ushered into the courtroom, where an overwhelming crowd of 250 filled the spectators' gallery. Some who were left in the hall grumbled that the two women "had pulled a fast one" to gain seats.

Serenading the seated gallery were the sounds of a coronet, wafting through the courtroom's open windows. A member of the Fireman's Band, practicing in the nearby Fulton Street engine house, produced the pleasing brass melodies.

Chester hoped to wrap up the prosecution Tuesday, but first he had the hurdle of getting past what the defense was now calling the "alleged confession." The issue centered on a jailhouse interview with Snook that Chester arranged for journalists 11 hours after the accused signed the "alleged confession" for police, then repudiated it. As Ricketts explained it, his client was still under duress as a result of the 22 hours of questioning at police headquarters when Snook gave reporters an interview in his cell. No defense attorney was present.

Anticipating a battle over the issue, Judge Scarlett put Franklin County Law Librarian Rudy Wittenmeir to work researching the proper authority on confessions, obtained under duress or otherwise. Surrounded by 36 law and reference books, the jurist then spent weekend hours examining the statutes.

The arguments began shortly after William C. Howells of *The (Cleveland) Plain Dealer* took the witness stand for the prosecution. He and James C. Fusco of *The Columbus Citizen* had conducted the midnight interview with Snook. Before Howells could begin his testimony, however, Ricketts strenuously objected, turning beet red in the process. He maintained, as he had before, that the defendant's statement to the press was part and parcel of the "alleged confession" given to the prosecutor and the police a few hours earlier. It was, he said, "obtained through fear [and] duress" and was involuntary without benefit of counsel.

Chester fought back just as vigorously while the jury was out of the courtroom. He made no effort to introduce the confession Snook signed for police, preferring to stick with what Snook told the reporters. Chester argued that Snook had met with Seidel.

"Yes, about two or three minutes," Ricketts responded sharply. "Seidel was run out and immediately afterward the defendant was assaulted by Chester," which the prosecutor acknowledged, noting that he had apologized for slapping Snook.

Judge Scarlett asked the Ricketts if he had any witnesses. "None that I want to use," the attorney replied.

Chester laughed. "Why don't you put him on the stand?" he asked, pointing to Snook, seated nearby. Ricketts did not respond.

After considerable argument, the jury returned, and testimony resumed.

More than 20 reporters were at the jail, Howells said, but only he and Fusco, representing all the others, were permitted back to Snook's cell. During his testimony, Howells referred to notes he took during the interview, although some viewed it as unusual for a reporter to just happen to have 2-month-old notes with him in court.

Snook, who told the reporters that he did not "have much more to say other than what was in my confession," responded amiably to the questions on a wide range of subjects. For example, he said that Theora was not a drug addict nor did she drink liquor, that she had shown considerable interest in literature on sex, that he had hurt his right hand repairing his automobile, that he was afraid she would carry out her threat to harm his wife and child, and that the last thing he remembered she said to him: "Damn you, I will kill you, too!"

As for the attack itself, Howells recalled that Snook said he struck the first blow with the flat side of the hammer when she grabbed for her purse on the seat beside her. The victim fell out of the car to escape his repeated blows, the hardest one using the ball end of the hammerhead.

Howells asked what happened next. Snook replied:

> She was unconscious and moaning. I didn't want her to suffer, as she had my sympathy. I didn't want to hit her on the head anymore. I hated to do that.

Snook continued, admitting that he could not say why he cut her throat, Howells said. What was the position of her body? asked the reporter. "She was lying on her back when I cut the vein."

Why didn't he go to the police? Howells wanted to know.

"I couldn't gather myself together to tell anything about the struggle," Snook responded, adding that he still loved his wife. With that, Chester concluded his examination of his witness. The prosecution had achieved its goal: getting into the trial Snook's "confession" to the reporters, rather than having to battle the defense over the admission of Snook's "confession" to police.

Seyfert conducted the cross-examination, focusing briefly on Howells' questioning Snook on his relationship with his wife. From his notes the reporter recalled that Snook said the question of divorce had never been discussed these and that there was never any serious dissension between the two.

Did she suspect he was having an affair? Howells asked the accused.

"I think she surmised I went out someplace, but she didn't know Miss Hix by name or by sight. Her name was never mentioned between us, I am sure of that."

Seyfert wanted Howells to describe Chester's voice volume during the questioning of Snook behind a locked door at police headquarters. "He has spoken louder here [in the courtroom] then he did over there," the reporter said. In any event, it was hard to distinguish individual voices, he said. No matter how hard he tried, Seyfert could not get the journalist to say he had overheard anything of substance.

Thursday afternoon, June 20, Chester showed Howells Snook's signed confession, which he said was "for use after midnight." The news that a confession had been obtained was published earlier in the day by *The Columbus Evening Dispatch*, thanks to the Shellenbarger news leak.

During his cross-examination Seyfert tried mightily to find out what the reporters saw and heard while his client was being questioned by Chester and others. He was convinced that the journalists were peeping through keyholes and placing their ears up against doors. He got very little from either Howells or Fusco, who employed other tactics.

What became clear from the testimony was that police headquarters and the county jail were deliciously porous for eager investigative reporters. The press had easy access to virtually everything that was transpiring during the investigation. None was present during the interrogation of Snook, but it made little difference. Again and again reporters tapped their "sources" for details while just hanging out with cops, jailers and attorneys more than willing to reveal what they knew.

After the midnight jail interview, Fusco testified that he briefly returned to Snook's cell with Sheriff Paul to ask three more questions posed by the reporters waiting outside.

"Are you sorry you killed Miss Hix?" The prisoner replied, "I am."

"Do you feel justified that you killed Miss Hix?" "No, I do not," Snook answered.

"Will you plead guilty to a charge of first-degree murder?"

Snook's immediate response was, "What else can I do?" Then, on reflection, he told Fusco: "Don't use that. I will have to see my attorneys."

At the end of his cross-examination, Seyfert asked Fusco "if you didn't see Mr. Ricketts trying to force open the door [to Chief French's anteroom] on Thursday morning, the door at the end of the corridor?" The reporter said he didn't see it, but Ricketts had tried to gain entry. The question sparked a comment from Chester that he knew would get Ricketts' goat.

"I would suggest, Mr. Ricketts, if you want to testify, take the stand here. It would be more becoming and be more ethical."

"I think we have the right to cross-examine and cross-examine in our own way," the elder defense attorney said, fuming.

"Proceed," said Judge Scarlett.

"I am just as ethical as you are!" Ricketts blustered.

"Thank you," said the prosecutor.

For spectators who had experienced long hours in line and in the courtroom, the testimony this day must have been a disappointment. Snook said nary a word and for most of the day only his all-but-bald spot could be seen by the gallery. At adjournment, Chester promised the Court he would rest his case Tuesday morning after one more witness.

Two downtown motion-picture theaters, both featuring the new "talkies," offered to host the jury panel Monday and Tuesday nights.

At the Loew's Broad Monday, the panel viewed *Bulldog Drummond,* starring Ronald Colman in "the greatest talking picture ever produced." The jurors sat in the first row of the loge and the deputy sheriffs and bailiffs in the second row. The following night at the Loew's Ohio, the jury would see Renée Adoree and William Collier Jr. in *Tide of Empire*, promoted as "a truly great sound thriller."

A real-life thriller was yet to be played out in the Franklin County Courthouse.

11 | THE STOOLIE

Snook rather enjoyed having a cellmate for a couple of weeks. Charles Carey was his name, but the police called him "stoolie."

Jailed for forgery shortly before Snook's arrest, Carey pleaded guilty to the charge. However, before he headed to the Ohio State Reformatory at Mansfield to do his time, he performed a little favor for the law -- more specifically, for Howard Lavely.

Lavely was a Franklin County detective assigned to the prosecutor's office and the Snook case. He also was the final witness for the prosecution on Tuesday morning, August 6, before another packed courtroom.

Despite being on crutches, Iva McAtee hopped up the stairs to the third floor to be among the earliest in line for court. Harry E. Gilmore of St. Louis, Missouri, arrived at 1:30 a.m. to be first. Once again Edward Clark was there also, keeping his string alive for having attended every session.

Juror 6, W. L. Balthaser, settled into his chair for another long day. All was well, now that he had the pillow he had requested for his jury chair.

Because he found the murder weapons, namely the ball-peen hammer and Snook's pocketknife, Lavely's testimony was important to the State's case. The hammer he recovered from a large toolbox in the defendant's basement a week after the murder. The knife, found at the same time, was in a smaller toolbox on a workbench, the witness said.

The following day Lavely visited Snook in jail and unwrapped the newspaper he had put around the hammer and the knife. "I asked him if those were the ones he used, and he said, 'Yes, those are the ones.'"

Lavely said he kidded Snook: "Doctor, you didn't wash them off very good, did you?" According to the witness, Snook agreed, telling the detective, "I just took them over [to] the built-in tubs in the basement and turned the water on." It never crossed his mind that they would be discovered, and a chemist would find blood on them.

At Chester's direction, Lavely showed each weapon to the jury, pointing out the spots of discoloration from blood. He then was turned over to Seyfert for cross-examination.

The defense questioning began with Lavely's participation in the questioning of Marion T. Meyers, who was at one time under suspicion but proved his innocence. While Lavely testified Tuesday morning, Meyers appeared in the courthouse, accompanied by his attorney, D. N. Postlewaite. After Meyers conferred with Seidel in a private room, he left the building, having been told that it was unlikely he would be needed as a defense witness.

Seyfert shifted his questioning to the day of Snook's arrest. Lavely was at police headquarters when the accused was brought in and asked "routine questions" in the detective bureau. "Doctor Snook denied at that time that he had anything to do with it [the murder]," the detective said. Later in the day, Snook faced questioning by a battery of law officers, including Chester. Nevertheless, Lavely recalled that the accused "varied very little from his original story," rocking back and forth on the rear legs of the straight-backed chair during the grilling.

The witness confirmed that Snook had been questioned "in relays," first by one officer, then another, then another.

"What did Dr. Snook say about the treatment that he was receiving or thought he was receiving at the hands of questioners," Seyfert asked.

"He thought it was a joke," Lavely said.

"Did you say anything to him in the way of cursing him or swearing at him?"

"Oh, I told him he wasn't a man, and I didn't think he was a man, and used several curse words in order to try to ruffle him or excite him," the witness said.

He repeated just what words he used. "I told him he was a dirty dog and a lot of other things that I don't remember." A few in the gallery snickered.

"As a matter of fact now, Mr. Lavely, didn't you call him a goddamn rat?" The witness hesitated, then replied, "I might have" and went on to acknowledge that there may have been others questioning Snook in the smoke-filled room who also used "pretty rough" language.

The cross-examination then turned to the prisoner known as Carey, a name that Lavely seemed to have difficulty remembering at first. In fact, the detective's memory failed him on many of the details, even though he admitted that he had Carey placed in Snook's cell. "I don't remember," he answered several times.

"And on whose orders or by whose authority was this man Carey ... placed in the same cell with Dr. Snook?"

"It was my own idea," Lavely said, even though he found it difficult to remember details of the incident barely two months earlier. He also testified that he did not tell his boss, Chester, about his plan until after he had placed the stoolie in the cell with Snook. When he did inform Chester, ["he] said it was all right," Lavely said.

"Now, Mr. Lavely, why did you have Charles Carey placed in the same cell with Dr. Snook?"

"I wanted to see his reactions and see what Dr. Snook would tell him."

Seyfert intimated that Carey had been granted a deal by the prosecutor's office, but Lavely denied it. He said he had done an unspecified favor for Carey, who now returned that favor.

"In other words you were trying to use a man who had been arrested on a forgery charge to repay you back by trying and attempting to pump Dr. Snook and sharing the same cell over there [for a couple of weeks] and seeing what he could drag or get out of Dr. Snook: Is that a fact?" Seyfert asked. Lavely agreed it was.

Although Seyfert implied that Lavely had found the two murder weapons in Snook's home as a result of information Carey provided, the detective denied the allegation. In fact, on the stand Lavely remembered very little of the information his stoolie gave to him.

On redirect of this witness, Chester asked if Snook's responses at police headquarters were "intelligent." Lavely agreed that they were.

"What about the answers as compared to some of the questions that were asked?"

"Sometimes he would, instead of answering the question, he would beat around the bush about it and tried to get your mind off what you were really asking," Lavely remembered.

"In other words," Chester said, "he was at all times trying to outsmart somebody else, wasn't he...? He was way ahead of everybody else who was doing the questioning most of the time."

"Yes, sir."

Chester concluded his case with the introduction of exhibits, including a 1928 photographic portrait of the attractive Theora Hix. The defense team objected to the attempt to gain the jury's sympathy for the deceased. The State had called 21 witnesses when it rested at 11:40 a.m. Now Chester had to wait and see if the defense put Snook on the stand, giving the prosecutor the opportunity to cross-examine the accused.

> *The evidence was quite immense*
> *Piled up by Chester's crew.*
> *It had the knife that spilled her life,*
> *And bloodstained hammer, too.*
> **George Tucker,** *The Columbus Evening Dispatch*

The defense opened its case, such as it was, by calling to the stand its two most prominent witnesses, Dr. David S. White, dean of the College of Veterinary Medicine since 1897, and Dr. Oscar V.

Brumley,[20] secretary of the college. Unfortunately, their testimony did little to help Snook's cause.

White recalled that Snook, as a respected professor at the college, was widely recognized for having modified "the roaring operation" that is performed on the larynx of a horse to prevent its making a roaring noise while gasping for air during a race. It is an operation that veterinarians still perform today. As to Snook's character, the white-haired White said it was "good."

Gessaman, in his cross-examination for the prosecution, asked the dean it he had ever "considered recommending the dismissal of Dr. Snook from the faculty of your college?" White said he had, about three months earlier, because he felt that Snook "was slipping somewhat in his work."

"Isn't it a fact, doctor, that you considered recommending to the president of the university his dismissal from the faculty of your college on account of his keeping company with women other than Mrs. Snook?"

"That was merely incidental, because I knew only of that by a vague rumor." He said Dr. Brumley had conveyed the rumor to him about two weeks before the murder occurred.

White left the witness stand after one more question:

> Wasn't Snook dismissing his clinical classes early, going to his office for 10 or 15 minutes and appearing late to his own classes?

"Yes," White admitted.

Brumley, who had been a prosecution witness earlier, was recalled to the stand and questioned by Gessaman about the rumor "in regard to his (Snook) association with women other than Mrs. Snook." Brumley said he had spoken to Snook about it about three years earlier. He also

---

[20] Snook was a contributor to Brumley's textbook, *Book of Veterinary Posology and Prescriptions*, Columbus, Ohio: R. G. Adams & Co, 1913, revised 1924. Posology is the study of drug medicines.

said he had warned Theora about associating with faculty, specifically professor Snook.

Because of the negative attention the case had drawn to Ohio State University and the apparent lack of decisive action on the part of White and Brumley, President Rightmire himself came under fire from students, parents, faculty and especially the alumni. To deflect the criticism, Rightmire chose this day to issue a statement regarding the university's policy for employing faculty.

"Persons in whose record there is the least taint of moral delinquency are not even considered for teaching appointments," he said. "Where such delinquency develops after appointment, executive action at once follows. ... In employing men and women for its staff and the retaining old employees, the university takes the utmost precautions to assure itself of their moral probity as well as their intellectual fitness. This has always been its rigid policy and this policy will continue to be adhered to strictly."

Before the Court's Tuesday afternoon session concluded, several character witnesses were called to the stand to testify as to Snook's "moral probity." Raymond C. Bracken, a Columbus lumber dealer and a fellow member of the 1920 Olympic pistol-shooting team, described Snook's character as "the very best." He said he had met Theora once when he saw her shooting with Snook at the Columbus Revolver Club in the basement of the Columbus Hotel. Bracken thought Theora "a fair shot as beginners go." (Snook and Theora also visited the Shot Gun Club on King Avenue, near the campus, and the university's range.)

Former state veterinarian Dr. Fred Zimmer of Pataskala, Charles A. Snow, a neighbor to the Snooks, and Dr. Howard W. Miller, a classmate of Snook's at the College of Veterinary Medicine and a Columbus city councilman, also took the stand as defense witnesses. All agreed that Snook had been "a peaceable man" as far as they knew.

12 | MOTHER AND WIFE

"There's his wife!" "Look! That's Mrs. Snook!"

Wednesday's visitors gallery stirred to life as Helen Snook, accompanied by attorneys Seyfert and E J. Schanfarber, made her first appearance in the courtroom, taking a seat at the defense table. When her husband entered moments later, she extended her hand to him. He held it endearingly; they kissed and sat side by side.

They had been together the night before when she and his mother briefly visited him in jail. With them for the first time was Mary Marple Snook, the couple's 2-year-old daughter, who Snook had not held since his arrest June 15.

Snook did not see his mother come into the courtroom inasmuch as she arrived through a gate behind him. When she reached the defense table, she threw her arms around his neck and smothered him with kisses. It caught him off-guard. He tried to get out of his chair to reciprocate, but her embrace did not allow it.

Helen was understandably nervous. Seyfert offered her water in a paper cup. "Take it easy now, Mrs. Snook," the attorney advised. "There is nothing to be afraid of." She nodded, removing her fur-trimmed coat to reveal a fetching georgette dress of pure white. A hat of natural straw color with a green band hid much of her face. White kid shoes and white gloves completed her ensemble. From the jury box, Mrs. Cassady smiled sympathetically at the witness. Snook fidgeted.

Ricketts led his soft-spoken witness – several times Judge Scarlett asked her to speak up – through her experiences as a sixth-grade teacher, wife and mother. She described her husband as "quiet, even-tempered" and never abusive. However, during the past two years or so, she described him as "restless."

Ricketts wanted the jury to know about her experience at police headquarters, where Shellenbarger, French and Chester questioned her five days after the murder. Present, also, was co-defense attorney Seidel, but "he was asked to leave," she said. "Mr. Chester told me that he felt I should have an attorney of my own, that Mr. Seidel was Dr. Snook's attorney and not mine." Attorney Schanfarber was called to police headquarters. He had represented her two years earlier when she inquired about a divorce.

For five hours Chester led the interrogation, Mrs. Snook said. "I was accused of the murder."

"Who made this accusation?"

"Mr. Chester.... He wanted to know if I knew that there was [sic] strands of hair found in the girl's hand that resembled mine in texture and color, and that they also found a paring knife that had been taken from my kitchen, and that I was guilty."

She said she broke down. "I told him I never did; never, never!" She pounded her fist on the arm of the witness chair. Her voice rose and shook. Close to tears, she retrieved a linen handkerchief from the small tapestry bag in her lap. "It just came with such a shock to me."

When Chester had the opportunity to cross-examine the witness, he carefully walked her through what he believed to be the circumstances surrounding the interrogation. "I asked you if you had anything to do with the murder; I said that a lot of people thought you might have on account of the fact that a lot of hairs were found in the girl's right-hand, isn't that right?"

"I think it was more direct than that, Mr. Chester," the former schoolteacher said sternly.

"All right, afterward it was, I will admit…. then it was shortly after that that you broke down and cried." That was true, she said.

The final two questions for Mrs. Snook were posed by Ricketts on re-direct: "I will ask you if you knew of his relations, if he had any such relations, with Theora Hix, deceased?"

"Absolutely no."

"Did you ever hear her name mentioned?"

"No."

The accused held the chair for his wife as she sat next to him once again. They smiled at one another.

The next witness to take the stand was quickly identified by the gallery: "That's his mother," the all-knowing whispered to their neighbors. A few hours earlier Mary E. Snook of Lebanon, Ohio, had not expected to be called to testify – her son did not want her to do so – but she insisted. After a brief conference between the three defense attorneys, they agreed to call her for the defense.

Taking the witness stand, the 73-year-old grandmother appeared calm, although she had been crying before entering the courtroom, a new experience for her. "I never wanted to be in a courtroom," she told reporters. "I am trying so hard to keep myself together so I won't break down. I must be able to talk in the witness stand."

The gallery of predominantly women noticed that she was well-turned-out in a black-and-white silk print dress, black horsehair hat, black shoes, tan gloves and a long black silk coat trimmed with a fur neckpiece, even in summer. She was ready for Ricketts' gentle questioning. Occasionally waving a fan to stir the air, she recalled in some detail her son's early life down on the farm in South Lebanon. (After the death of her husband, she had moved off the farm and to nearby Lebanon in 1926.)

"Just a minute," Chester said, standing tall. "I don't know the purpose of putting Mrs. Snook on the stand. If it is for the purpose of a character witness, that is perfectly all right, we have no objection. If it is for any other purpose, I think that counsel ought to state so at this time. I cannot see any materiality in this testimony."

Mrs. Snook began to reply: "I just feel that I want to..."

"I am not talking to you," the prosecutor interrupted. After a brief, spirited debate between opposing attorneys, Judge Scarlett allowed the questioning to continue.

As a lad on the farm, Snook gained an interest in hunting, fishing and shooting. The future Olympic shooting champion had a gun (a rifle) of his own. "The first money he earned he took it and bought him a little gun," she said. "He was very proud of it because he earned it himself." Ricketts asked whether Snook spent his time "out with the boys in town."

The question brought tears to the eyes of the witness. "Oh, no, no; he was a home boy," she stated, repeatedly dabbing her eyes with her linen handkerchief. Her son was visibly upset, also. Showing emotion was out of character for him.

It was Judge Scarlett who interrupted next. "It seems to me a good deal of this is entirely irrelevant," he said. Chester quickly agreed. The testimony petered out, and she was excused. As she left the stand, she stopped to grasp her son's hand. He rose. The eyes of both mother and son were filled with tears. Many women in the gallery were affected by the tragic scene.

Although her daughter-in-law remained in the courtroom, Mrs. Snook retired to an adjoining room to "wait for Helen." She trembled as she wept softly, comforted by Mrs. Lilly Landrum, Helen Snook's cousin from Junction City, Ohio.

What came next was what thousands of newspaper readers and several hundred courtroom spectators had been waiting for: the "dirt" from the defendant's own lips.

"The defendant may take the stand," Ricketts said, matter-of-factly.

13 | IN HIS DEFENSE – PART I

"I do," a stoic Snook calmly responded after Criminal Court Clerk Joseph H. Palmer completed the "to tell the truth" oath. The doors of justice were about to open wide on details surrounding what New York journalist James L. Kilgallen described as "one of the most sordid murder trials ever staged in an American courtroom."

For breathless spectators who attended the trial and thousands of newspaper readers who passionately followed every word of it, this was what they had been itching for – "the dirt" from the mouth of the accused. Little did the newspaper readers know, however, that they would never read the steamy side of Snook's testimony. Editors universally found it to be beyond the realm of public decency.

The gallery began arriving at midnight Tuesday, lining up for a coveted seat in the third-floor courtroom. Mrs. Lela Shelton brought a camp chair, coffee in a thermos and a sandwich in a cracker box to ease the long wait, but she rarely had a chance to sit down. The crowd standing around her was too dense. She had brought a friend, but when the courthouse doors finally opened, the two women became separated in the stampede. The crowd "galloped up two flights of stairs like mountain goats," a *Columbus Citizen* reporter wrote. Mrs. Shelton found a seat inside, but her friend did not.

Harry E. Gilmore, a railroad brakeman from St. Louis, secured a seat. His attendance testified to the widespread interest in the case. "I just had to come see for myself, 'cause I've heard too much about it," he told reporters. Sidney S. Taylor of Hot Springs, Arkansas, and Hubert E. Denlinger of Philadelphia also were among those who attended from afar.

Theora's parents, Dr. and Mrs. Melvin Hix, read magazines and newspapers in Chester's offices and waited for news from the trial.

As Seyfert began his examination of the lanky former professor, Ricketts and Seidel slipped out of the courtroom to grab a smoke, missing Snook's description of his early life in South Lebanon and his subsequent 19 years as an instructor in veterinary medicine at Ohio State University. Seyfert also explored Snook's expertise as a pistol shot, both as a national title-holder and as a double Olympic gold-medal winner. Then Seyfert popped the question everyone was waiting for.

"Now, doctor, when was the first time that you ever met Miss Theora Hix?" Helen Snook quietly but quickly left the courtroom to join her mother-in-law. Accompanied by Schanfarber, the two women departed the courthouse together through a back door. Mrs. Minnie Ricketts and her 19-year-old daughter, Helen – the one who had been threatened earlier – also left at the suggestion of her husband.

In a firm, unwavering voice full of confidence, Snook testified that he first encountered Theora in June 1926 when she worked as a stenographer at the veterinary college, taking dictation for a number of professors. He was 46; she was 21.

One rainy day he gave her a ride to Mack Hall, a women's campus dormitory. Snook said he did not know if she knew at the time that he was a married man.

Within the next few days and in the weeks beyond, they had many conversations and many rides in his automobile, he said. Subjects for discussion included intercourse, venereal disease and "companionate marriage," akin to a common-law marriage. "It was along about that time," Snook said, "that she said she preferred someone older, who really knew something."

"When was the first time you and Miss Hix had sexual relations?" Seyfert asked matter-of-factly. Spectators sat up straighter, straining to hear the response.

"Probably within ... three or four weeks after I met her. "Initial intercourse took place in a rented room "somewhere on the east side" over a period of three hours, Snook said. Their pillow talk centered on sex, and it appeared to him that "she knew more about sex affairs than I did," he admitted somewhat sheepishly. For example, she already had read *The Art of Love* which he subsequently purchased for her. "Quite a rare book," the witness said.

During the summer of 1926, Snook taught Theora how to shoot both a .22-caliber Winchester rifle and a .22-caliber Smith & Wesson single-shot pistol. When she told him she had been frightened by a prowler outside her first-floor room in Mack Hall, he gave her a .41-caliber Remington derringer for protection. "It hits quite hard," he admitted.

Although the couple was meeting for intercourse two or three times a week, Theora began having another relationship – with Marion Meyers, meeting with him two or three times a week as well. Snook said she would tell him intimate details of what she and Meyers did while together; presumably she also told bedroom stories when with Meyers.

(It came out during Snook's testimony that police had arrested Theora and Meyers for having intercourse while parked on the River Road along the Scioto River. Both were charged and fined $20 apiece. Theora gave police a fake name, Marian Thorn.)

Chester objected to this line of testimony, pointing out that Meyers ceased his relationship with Theora in the fall of 1928 because he became engaged to another. Ricketts argued that the jury should have "all the facts." He wanted to paint Theora as "a two-woman man." Seyfert immediately corrected his associate's malapropism to "a two-man woman."

Gesturing with a long sweep of his arm and holding up three fingers, Ricketts declared that "all three of them were, to a certain extent, insane!"

Judge Scarlett allowed the defense to continue its line of questioning, but just as he did so, he momentarily halted the proceedings because of noise from would-be spectators in the hallway. Irene Kuhn of the *New York Daily News* described the scene as "hundreds of shrieking, yelling men and women, loudly demanding admittance to the courtroom already stuffed to suffocation." The Court ordered Sheriff Paul and several bailiffs to clear the hallway of "the outsiders."

According to the former professor's recollection, Theora left for New York in early June 1928 with the stated intention of transferring to the Long Island Medical School. When that did not work out for her, she enrolled at Columbia University to make up a course in neurology that she had failed at Ohio State. She passed with an A. While in New York, she earned money as a typist for the International Scholarship Bureau, then returned to Columbus in September to begin her second year of medical school at Ohio State. She continued to date both Snook and Meyers regularly for intimate encounters.

While in New York, she had wired Snook several times, asking him to come to New York, but it was Ohio State Fair time, a large and popular annual event. Snook had responsibilities associated with the livestock on exhibit there, and he could not leave. In their first face-to-face meeting, Snook implored Meyers to go in his stead. "He said he wouldn't do that unless I would agree not to see her anymore, and I agreed," Snook said.

But in November Theora broke off her relationship with Meyers because he insisted upon getting married, Snook said. Within an hour after she telephoned Snook's office to tell him the news, they met and resumed their physical affair, meeting again two or three times a week for what Seyfert described as "simply natural sex relations."

Together, Snook said, they found an $8-per-week, third-floor, furnished room near S. High Street. For two months they met there in the evenings or on Saturday or Sunday afternoons. When they left the walk-up, they left separately – one out the front door and the other out the rear – and drove away in his car.

Over a period of some months, Snook lent Theora a total of $1,000 and established a savings account in her name. "She felt that [her sexual activity] might be found out and that if [it] was, she wanted to leave Columbus and leave in a hurry," Snook testified. "Well, I said, 'That'll be all right; you can buy a ticket and go.'" He admitted she paid the money back – plus the 6 percent interest he charged her.

At medical school in the fall of 1928, Theora took courses in medica and pharmacology. "So, it was sometime during those courses that she began taking drugs," Snook said, testing on herself the effects of various drugs, including cocaine twice. She also consumed a small greenish colored tablet: it was *Cannabis indica*, a form of marijuana. Snook said he had never seen it in tablet form before, only as a fluid extract used in the veterinary hospital.

There was a brief disturbance in the gallery. Frances Comer of Piketon swooned from the oppressiveness of the courtroom air. Friends took her to the restroom, where she regained her composure.

Defense attorney Seyfert asked Snook to describe one of the last times the two were together at the love nest in the spring of 1929. Snook fidgeted in the witness chair. For the first time he seemed uncomfortable.

"I couldn't do anything to please her; she didn't like the way I would do things," he said. They would frequently argue. "One time she said she wanted to hurt me or scratch me and referred to a statement in one of the books on sexology she had in which somebody said it always gave them a lot of satisfaction to scratch someone else."

Another time, Snook testified, she slapped a magazine out of his hand because he wasn't paying attention to her, then slapped his face with such force that his pince-nez cut his nose and flew across the room. The slapping occurred on several occasions, he said.

Snook was not the only one to suffer the repercussions of Theora's moods. She blackened Meyers' eye and then told Snook about it. Snook later observed the damage for himself.

Several times she became petulant, refusing to get out of his car. On one occasion, when he was on his way to care for a friend's horse, "she dared me to throw her out," he said. "She said if I did... she would go up to [his] house and make things hot for me up there."

Seyfert inquired about the fear Snook felt regarding the derringer he had seen in her purse several times. In other words, he tried to keep an eye on its whereabouts. "I felt she would not hesitate to use it on me when she would get angry like that," and her moments of anger increased in 1929.

"She began insisting upon seeing me more often," Snook said. "One night...she wouldn't get out of the machine," so they sat in the car from 9 p.m. until midnight with Theora doing all the talking. "She didn't want to go home, and she didn't feel like getting out and [she] cried about it and fussed around in that way." He recalled another occasion, when the argument in the car concerned his plans to spend a weekend with his mother in Lebanon. They drove the streets of Clintonville (a Columbus neighborhood just north of the university's campus) for three hours because "she wouldn't get out, and she dared me to throw her out."

For Snook by far the most embarrassing experience occurred Sunday afternoon, June 9, four days before the murder. He drove to the private Scioto Country Club – site of Bobby Jones' victory in the U.S. Open three years earlier – where he picked up a golf game with attorney Charles Sumner Druggan and his guest, former State Highway Commissioner Louis A. Boulay. As they were about to tee off, Tony Cocciadeferro emerged from the clubhouse and handed Snook a telephone number to call. Snook tried twice to do so because the deskman understood the caller – unidentified as to gender – to say that it was "very important." After getting no answer, Snook rejoined the other men and his 13-year-old caddie, Romeo "Romy" Scarpitti, on the first tee.

At the par 4, 430-yard fifth hole, Druggan sliced his drive into heavy rough. He found his ball just as Theora walked up to Snook. "She had a peculiar look in her eye," he said. "Her whole chin trembled, as if she was angry as she could be." She vociferously complained that he had not returned her call to the clubhouse and demanded that he immediately leave the course with her.

"She kept on talking, and Mr. Druggan was ready to shoot. I wanted to get her to keep still until he shot, and she said she didn't give a damn whether he shot or not." She refused his invitation to walk along with them as well as his suggestion that they meet after he finished nine holes. "'No,'" she said stridently, "'I want you to go right away! I mean it!'" She won the argument.

"Romy" said he picked up Snook's ball, and "me and him walked to the clubhouse" where Snook signed the caddie's card, earning Romy the caddy fee of $1.

Theora waited in the professor's coupe while Snook showered and changed clothes but then complained angrily that he took too long. They drove to the love nest, where she continued to pout. Little did she realize that by interrupting Snook's Saturday golf game, she had sealed her fate.

Judge Scarlett adjourned court for the day shortly thereafter, "just as we were getting to the good part," commented one spectator. Snook stepped down from the witness chair, grateful for the relief. He would be back on the stand Thursday morning.

A light dinner was on tap for the jurors, half of whom had been battling indigestion, including Mrs. Cassady. Special bailiff Mayme Weir, a registered nurse, attributed the malady to "sitting all day and eating heavy meals." Afterward the jurors came in for a real treat. They were entertained at the Southern Hotel by the "Singing Deputies." Franklin County Sheriff Harry Paul led the accomplished quintet that included his son, Ralph, William and Orland Everett and Robert Willison.

14 | IN HIS DEFENSE – PART II

Mrs. Mary Potter and her friend, Mrs. Carl Hutchison, both of nearby Worthington, were pleased with themselves when they arrived at the Franklin County Courthouse at 11 p.m. Wednesday. They discovered they were first in line for the hottest ticket in town. Fortune smiled on them again when in the wee hours of Thursday morning, a thoughtful courthouse janitor invited them to catch a nap in his automobile.

An elderly woman also gained a favor when she approached elevator operator William Trautman. "Is this where they are holding this Snook trial?" she asked.

It was, Trautman replied, "but I don't think you could get in." Already more than 200 anxiously waited in the hallway.

"Oh, I don't want to hear the trial," she said. "I just want to see the crowds trying to get in." Trautman took her up to the third floor for a gander, then back to the lobby.

When Snook again took the witness stand shortly after 9 a.m., he displayed the steadiness of a champion pistol shooter – but his trousers needed a press. Again defense attorney Seyfert conducted the interrogation. After a few warm up questions, he asked, "When was the first time your relations, sexually speaking, were unnatural with Miss Hix?"

Unnatural relations? Once again the spectators edged forward to hear every word of the testimony. "The first of April," the defendant replied positively.

Seyfert stumbled for words – delicate words.

"I just want you to relate now, Dr. Snook, as near as you can, without going into too many details, in a generalized way, just what took place at that time between you and Miss Hix."

Theora complained that his "performance" had not been up to snuff and "fussed" about not being satisfied, he testified. "Finally, she insisted that she be allowed to satisfy it the way she wanted to, and she did so by taking my privates in her mouth; and that was the first time."

There was an audible shift in positions in the sweltering courtroom. Blushing men and women avoided glancing at one another. One woman spectator fainted. In the jury box, Mrs. Cassady lowered her head slightly, shielding her eyes under a wide-brimmed black hat. Raunchy details such as this were too explicit to publish in the newspapers.

"Even the tabloid writers were stumped Thursday," wrote Mary V. Daugherty of *The Ohio State Journal*. "They got what they had been asking for in the way of testimony and found they couldn't write it."

A hush came over the courtroom as Dr. Snook began his recounting of the events June 13, the day of the murder. He described his meeting Theora at 12th and High streets about 8 p.m., shortly after he had purchased a loaf of rye bread and some hamburger meat to take home for "the usual late lunch." Off they went in his blue Ford coupe.

"We drove north [on High Street] to Lane Avenue, west on Lane Avenue across the [Olentangy] river, out one of those roads, back and forth and finally hit Lane Avenue again at the entrance of Upper Arlington Road [Avenue] near the corner of Scioto Golf Club."

"She asked me if I had eaten anything, and I told her no, and she said that she had; she looked for me and didn't see me as she was a little bit early, and she stopped and had a bite to eat, and she said, 'I brought you a sandwich.'" He said he ate it while driving along Lane Avenue, tossing the crusts out the window.

Snook continued. "We talked about my going to Lebanon...and she asked me to make it [the trip] as quick as I could."

They also discussed giving up the love nest, now that she would be busy with her new job as a telephone switchboard operator. As they drove west from the campus area, Snook spotted lights on at the country club, so, he said, he stopped to visit his locker and get the yellow-tinted glasses he wore while shooting and playing golf. Theora waited for him in the car.

The lovers drove north from the club, stopping alongside the Scioto River, but "there were several machines there, and she said, 'Well, this doesn't look good to me. I'd like to go someplace farther where I can scream.'" Snook suggested they drive farther north along the river, but Theora said she was afraid to go there. "Then I told her I knew about this rifle range... [that] was rather secluded. She'd not been to that one before. After we'd turned down the road, she asked me if I was feeling better. That was a common expression that she made to me, and moved over closer to me and put her hand on my knee ... [then] she put her arm around my shoulder."

"Dr. Snook, what conversation did you have after you parked the car?"

"I asked her what she thought of this place. She said it was all right – 'seemed dark enough.' I told her it was a side road and didn't expect anyone to drive by if we should hurry. I asked her if she would get out of the machine or inside, and she said, 'Let's try it inside.' We'd never tried it in the new machine before."

"You are speaking of sexual intercourse?" asked Seyfert.

"Yes."

According to Snook, they engaged in sex in the car, but the space was incredibly cramped, and Snook had no prophylactics. "We made the best of it," withdrawing early, Snook said, but admitting it was "unsatisfactory for both of us." The couple resumed their seats, but

Theora was unhappy. "She said, 'It isn't much of a machine,' implying I should have a larger machine that would be more convenient" for sex.

Snook started the engine, but Theora reached over and turned it off, refusing to leave. Suddenly, she changed the subject, he said, telling him, "'You are not going home [to Lebanon] over the weekend.' I said: 'I have to go. I have told my mother I would be there.' And she said: 'Damn your mother! I don't care about your mother! You must not go!' My next remark was in regard to the work I was to do and that Mrs. Snook was expecting me to go."

"'Damn Mrs. Snook,' she said. 'I am going to kill her and get her out of the way!'"

Snook slowly removed his pince-nez and broke into tears. The courtroom fell silent a full minute, save for the ticking of the wall clock.

Urged by his attorney to continue, Snook testified that Theora shouted at him: "'Damn the baby. I will kill her, too.'" Again Snook broke down. He wiped his eyes with a handkerchief. Those in the jury box watched silently.

Snook continued. Theora demanded his attention once again, he said. Almost nonstop the witness recalled what Theora had said: "'You have got to help me out,' and with that she grabbed open my trousers, which had been buttoned up, and went down on me then, and she didn't do it very nicely, and she bit me and grabbed my right hand and got a hold of my privates and pulled so hard I simply could not stand it, and I tried to choke her off, and I couldn't get her loose that way, and then I grabbed her left arm and gave it a twist, and finally pulled her loose, partly, and she grabbed back again, and all I could do was to hold her head up close to keep her from hurting me, and [I turned] around and I got hold of something out of this [tool] kit and hit her with it, and I didn't hit her very hard. I finally got her loose and twisted her away – very nearly twisted her arm off, I thought, to make her get up in the machine. She sat there a little bit and she said: 'Damn you! I will kill you, too.'"

Few in the gallery drew a breath. Mouths were agape. Fellatio? In Columbus, Ohio? In a Ford coupe? Snook paused, removed his glasses

Theora K. Hix. Reprinted, with permission, from *The Columbus Dispatch Archives: Acme Newspictures Collection*

Mrs. Helen Snook stood by her husband to the end. Reprinted, with permission, from *The Columbus Dispatch*

At his trial, Snook is surrounded by (l-r) Sheriff Harry Paul, defense attorneys John E. Seidel and E. O. Ricketts, and trial prosecutor John J. Chester, Jr. Reprinted, with permission, from *The Columbus Dispatch*

Dr. and Mrs. Melvin Hix at the trial. Reprinted, with permission from *The Columbus Citizen*, Scripps Howard Newspapers/Grandview Heights Public Library/Photohio.org

Hundreds jammed the courthouse hallways for a chance to attend Snook's trial. Reprinted, with permission, from *The Columbus Dispatch*

Chemists look for evidence in Snook's 1929 blue Ford coupe.
Reprinted, with permission, from *The Columbus Dispatch*

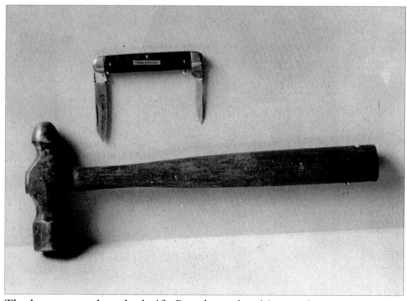

The hammer and pocketknife Snook used as his murder weapons.
Reprinted, with permission, from *The Columbus Dispatch*

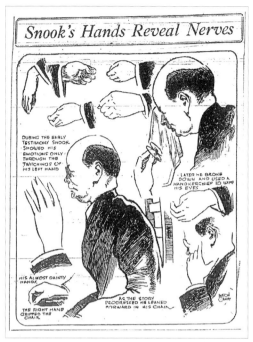

Famed comic strip cartoonist Milton Caniff captured images of the Snook trial for *The Columbus Evening Dispatch.* Reprinted with permission of the Milton Caniff estate

This little booklet containing salacious trial testimony sold briskly until police halted sales. Courtesy of Nick Taggart.

James Howard Snook's official Ohio Penitentiary photograph was hung on the wall of the death chamber after his execution. Courtesy Charles C. Howard.

and wiped away a tear with his handkerchief. The Court waited. The sounding of a loud automobile horn in the street broke through the silence.

Seyfert asked, "What else, if anything, did she say to you at that time, doctor?"

"Well, she said, 'Damn you! I will kill you, too,' and then she started out of the machine, grabbed for her purse and …slid out of the machine, and I was all doubled over; I couldn't straighten up, and I didn't realize what was happening. I had so much pain, and I tried to straighten up, and all at once it flashed in my mind that she was getting out, and I knew if she got out, she would shoot me."

"Where was her purse at that time, doctor?"

"She reached around – she turned her back to me and grabbed it, and I could not see where she got it. I think she got it off of the shelf [behind the front seat]. I grabbed for her after she got about halfway out, and I pulled her back so that her head was right down on the cushion of the machine and I hit her once then, and [it] apparently had no effect. I could not hit her – it seemed like I was not strong enough – and I hit her again and she slid right on down, out on the ground, and I followed her out. I couldn't get up. I couldn't raise my legs up. I just crawled out and fell out, and we both were out on the ground about the same time.

"She got up, hanging onto the door, and I got up behind her. I reached for the purse again, and she turned her back to me, and I hit her once more with the hammer, and she went down and hit her head against the running board of the machine. That put her to my left, and she kept hanging onto the door all the time.… As she fell, the door went shut and her head and neck somewhere hit the running board, and that is as near as I know about it."

After that, Snook could remember very little of the incident except to say: "I'm sure that I didn't hit her but three times in the machine and once when she got out. I can't imagine any more licks with the hammer than that. I couldn't straighten up, and the next thing I know, I was sitting on the running board of the machine, doubled over with my elbows on my knees."

The first, "not very hard" blows Snook described were to get her to let loose of him, the third and fourth were because he thought that she would kill him. He had taught her to use the derringer. If she ever got in trouble on a date, she was to shoot from the hip.

Seyfert asked, "Did you think and believe that Miss Hix, when she said she would kill your wife and child, actually meant to do it?" He did.

"At any time that night out there when you struck the first, second, third or last blow, I will ask you whether, Dr. Snook, you intended at all to kill Theora Hix?"

"I don't know!" the witness cried, holding his head in his hands once again as he sobbed. "Heavens knows, she was a good friend of mine. I never thought she would do it - that I would do it."

The Court declared a recess so Snook could compose himself. Seemingly, everyone caught their breath at one time after having held it for so long. The distraught defendant continued to weep while resting in the sheriff's office.

On the second floor, in Chester's office, the prosecutor told reporters that Ricketts had "come to me repeatedly and asked if I would consent to a plea of first-degree murder with mercy, and I refused him." Such a plea would allow Snook to escape the electric chair. Chester said he had "asked Ricketts why he didn't plead his client guilty to first-degree murder rather than to permit all this smut and dirt to come before the public." Ricketts refused to do so, he said.

As for Snook's testimony, "He's doing fine as far as I'm concerned," Chester said. "I couldn't ask for anything better."

After 15 minutes Snook had pulled himself together and the trial resumed. Seyfert asked his witness, "What did you do after you found yourself sitting on the running board of the automobile?"

"Why, I was sitting there, stooped over and crying, tears running down my face. I saw the girl laying [sic] there, and I spoke to her, and I didn't get any reply. I raised up and looked around, and that is the first time I realized somebody might come around there, so – I don't know just how I got into the machine, but I got in and hurried away."

"Did you cut her jugular vein?"

"I do not know that I did."

Snook recalled that while driving home, he discovered Theora's purse on the seat beside him. "I realized I should not take it home. I threw it out" – over the Quarry Bridge.

On his way home, Snook stopped to purchase the evening paper, but he could not concentrate on it. He never opened the first page. He just stared at it while sitting at the kitchen table. His thoughts were elsewhere. About 10:30 p.m., Helen Snook came downstairs briefly, had a word or two with her husband, "but no conversation," the witness said. Shortly thereafter, he went to bed and slept until 8 a.m., "as usual."

Seyfert turned his attention to the bloodstained items the prosecution had introduced as State exhibits.

"Doctor, I will ask you to look carefully at this dress marked at State's Exhibit 1 and ask you if you have ever seen that dress before?" Snook said he was "pretty sure" Theora wore it the night she was killed. However, he could not account for the bloodstains on the garment or on several other items of clothing Seyfert held up for his client's examination.

The attorney also held up State's Exhibit 28, a pocketknife, for inspection and the notification. Snook admitted he had one like it that he had purchased at Sears, Roebuck.

"I will ask you, the night that you went to the range with Theora Hix, on the evening of June 13th, whether or not you had a pocket knife similar to this on your person?"

"I did."

"I will ask you whether or not you had that same knife the following morning at your home on W. 10th Avenue?"

"No. But I found it on the floor of the machine the next morning when I went to drive out ...That little hammer was down there with it," pointing to State's Exhibit 39 on the table with the others items. Both tools he rinsed off and put away in the basement, he said.

Seyfert suddenly threw his client a curve with a single question about the severing of Theora's jugular vein.

"Dr. Snook, if Theora Hix' left jugular vein was cut and her carotid artery severed, I will ask you whether or not, under oath, if you did use the knife, with one blade or the other or both, in severing that vein or that artery?"

"I do not know that I did." It was a response Snook used a number of times.

Seyfert asked him to recall his visit with Mrs. Smalley at the "love nest" the afternoon after the murder. Snook said he paid her $3, told "the old lady" that he was leaving, and left his key on the table in the room. "Then I realized that Miss Hix probably would not be back, because school was over, and she would not have to study anymore, and I went back and unlocked the door and left the other key."

Snook had stated the obvious: Theora would not have to study anymore.

The defense attorney delved deeply into the conduct of police and the prosecutor during their interrogation of his client in Chief Shellenbarger's office at police headquarters. The chief led the questioning initially, the witness said, but then others joined in: Chester, detectives Phillips, Van Skaik and McCall, and the prosecution's investigator, Lavely. The questioning lasted for more than seven hours before Snook was taken to the county jail for the night. There he gave a deputy sheriff money to buy a sandwich and coffee – the first food he had since his breakfast with Van Skaik.

Although Snook was held in custody while the investigation continued, the intense questioning in Shellenbarger's office did not begin anew until Wednesday afternoon, June 19. First one officer of the law would question Snook, then another. It continued virtually nonstop through the night until about 7 a.m. the following day. "Lunch" for Snook was a sandwich, an orange, and a half pint of milk.

"Now, did anyone curse you that evening, doctor? Seyfert asked.

"Yes, quite a bit," the witness replied. His attorney asked him to describe what was said.

"Detective Phillips and Lavely did most of it and moved up close, sat on the table facing me, right up to within 2 or 3 feet, and talked in a loud tone of voice and told me practically all the cuss words that I ever heard and every other dirty reference that they could make to me in every way possible." There were also threats, he said, such as "that I should be stretched up and hung, and I should be electrocuted."

Detectives Phillips and McCall returned Snook to the county jail, stopping at a restaurant for breakfast. Snook slept soundly for about an hour, only to be called out to meet in a jail anteroom with Chester, Shellenbarger and French. They wanted him to confess, but he first wanted to see Seidel, his attorney. After a two-minute conference, the law officers called Snook back, telling him, "Now, you have seen him, go ahead and talk."

"I told them that I didn't have any story to tell," Snook said, at which point Seidel entered the room. "Prosecutor Chester ordered him out, pushed him out and slammed the door shut."

"What happened immediately after Mr. Seidel left that room there?"

"Prosecutor Chester came back and hit me on the side of the face three times on each side and knocked my glasses off."

"What did he say, if anything, to you at that time that he struck you in the face?"

"Oh, he cursed me some way. I think he said: 'Now damn it,' or 'Damn you. Go ahead and tell the story. You've got to tell it. We know that you know more, and you must tell it.'"

"Did he strike you with his open hand or with his closed fist?"

"I think it was his closed fist on either side of the head, because it shook me up quite a bit, and my glasses flew off halfway across the room."

Both French and Shellenbarger watched without comment,[21] Snook said. Stenographer Brown also witnessed the incident.

Shortly thereafter, Shellenbarger and McCall drove Snook back to police headquarters where the interrogation began again behind locked doors. Again the defendant said he felt threatened by curses from

---

[21] By some accounts, Chief French interceded, telling Chester "there's no need for that," but Snook did not recall that comment.

Phillips and Lavely, who suggested a lynching at Broad and High streets.

Once again Snook removed his pince-nez to wipe away a tear.

Finally, after more than four hours of hammering questions from "the whole bunch," Chester asked Snook to dictate his "confession" to a court stenographer. "I started to dictate it, and I couldn't say anymore … so prosecutor Chester added to that and dictated a full confession to the stenographer."

"Did you sign any so-called confession at that time?"

"I signed on that book that the stenographer wrote down. It was in shorthand, and I can't read shorthand, and that is the only signature that I put down."

So, after hours of intense interrogation in a smoke-filled room, a lack of sleep and nourishment and a "hit on the side of the head that didn't help very much," Snook succumbed.

His ordeal was not over, however. Back in his cell, he quickly fell asleep only to be awakened at midnight Thursday by a delegation of reporters seeking an interview. They said they had been "sent over from police headquarters, and I told them I didn't have anything to say. Well, they said they insisted on it because they wanted more information about the confession. … So, I couldn't very well do otherwise."

Seyfert ended his direct examination with a few questions concerning bloodstains on various items of his and Theora's clothing, a box of .41 caliber short cartridges and the derringer pistol he had given her in July of 1926.

"It is not loaded, is it?" Judge Scarlett asked with considerable self amusement.

"That is what I wanted to know," Chester said jocularly.

"The State is apparently getting scared," Seyfert observed.

15 | LETTERS FROM MABEL

Chester's snapping dark eyes focused on his target sitting in the witness chair. Ladies in the courtroom craned their necks and rose on their toes as they eagerly awaited the curtain to go up on the next act of a licentious drama, the likes of which Ohio had never seen.

The casting had Chester as the good guy – tall and slim, dashing and impulsive – the epitome of the hero seeking justice. Snook – balding and squinty-eyed with glasses pinching his nose – represented the villainous, nerdy professor. Still, there were women who found a fascination with the charismatic, dimple-chinned Snook – as long as he didn't have a hammer in his hand.

Once again the crowd in the hallway, still several hundred strong, became unruly in its attempt to hear the testimony. The bailiffs tried to quiet them until Judge Scarlett told his officers to leave the would-be spectators alone.

Right off the bat, Chester tried to embarrass the witness and unnerve him. Referring to Snook's jailhouse interview with the reporters, he asked, "Do you remember the statement that you made to them in which you said you did not want to hide behind a woman's skirts?" Snook denied that he had made any statement like that.

"So, that you are perfectly willing to hide behind a woman's skirts, are you ... if it is necessary to save your life?"

Ricketts exploded with an objection.

"Oh, I suppose that is argumentative," said the judge, and Chester moved on to the derringer, asking Snook if it worked. "No," came the reply, "it does not cock... it could not be shot." It was a surprising admission from a man who claimed self-defense because he feared being shot by his paramour.

Did he, the prosecutor asked, ever go to Cleveland while Theora was attending Western Reserve University? Snook admitted he had gone twice in the summer of 1927, during the time Theora had the use of Marion Meyers' car. Eventually, she and Meyers drove it back to Columbus. Then Chester caught Snook off guard. It was a question that no one expected.

"Dr. Snook, do you know what a Steinach[22] operation is?"

"I do not."

"Did you ever perform a bisectomy?" Chester meant "vasectomy."

"Yes."

"Upon yourself?"

"Yes, sir."

"Explain to members of this jury what a bisectomy is."

"A severing of the duct that leads from the testicle up to the upper part of the ejaculatory duct that carried spermatozoa from the testicle up." A few spectators gasped. Chester pushed the line of questioning.

"Would you explain in just ordinary everyday language now what a bisectomy is and what the purpose of it is, just as though you were explaining to a class."

"Well, I don't know what the primary purpose is because that is out of my line, but I know why... "

---

[22] German scientist Eugen Steinach studied methods for sexual rejuvenation. His treatments, including surgery, were widely viewed as quackery.

With a look of incredulity on his face, the prosecutor interrupted the witness. "You say that you don't *know* what the primary purpose of a bisectomy is and yet you performed it upon yourself?"

"Just a minute…"

"Let him answer the question," Seyfert interjected.

Snook continued as though he was teaching a class in veterinary medicine. He explained that the operation would "cause atrophy of the testicle" and relieve any sensation or any enlargement of it. "There are two results of the operation; one is it prevents spermatozoa from passing out and naturally would prevent conception, and the other is it causes atrophy of the testicle, and it goes up farther and gets out of its usual position.…The testicle gets smaller."

Snook claimed that the sole reason he had performed the surgery on himself was to reduce the smaller testicle because it rubbed on his trousers, resulting in considerable discomfort. He said the sensitivity of the testicle was the result of having the mumps as a child. Later in the testimony, this surgery was referred to more accurately as a vasectomy.

The defense was caught off guard yet again when Chester introduced a packet of letters Snook had written to his lover after this self-applied surgery. The missives, found by Detective Gail McGrath while searching Theora's room, were descriptive and often vulgar, yet they were introduced over the objections of the defense, which had not been given access to them.

Chester elected to read excerpts from the letters. Many were written on *Hunter, Trader, Trapper* stationery and included self-addressed envelopes that Snook provided Theora for her replies. His began with endearments such as "My Dear Sweetkissikums" and "My Dearie." Snook also passed along "an earthquake tremor squeeze," "a kiss… à la Belmont[23] to hold you until the next letter," and "a little squeeze and a real kiss – high power only."

Snook underlined snippets he wanted to emphasize to his lover. This "sad part" pertained to the vasectomy:

---

[23] An apparent reference to silent film star Joseph "Baldy" Belmont.

Now, to come to the sad part of the letter. There is a chance I will not be able to come up. And if I do ... [I] may not be able then. You recall that I showed you a little place and had you feel it, and which, if severed, would prevent possible trouble. Well, I have been wanting to snip them both for sometime, and that was the plan that I had in mind when I wrote you of a plan that would carry over last weekend and this one, too. So, thinking this was a good time to try, I did fix the little one only; did it as soon as I came back [from Cleveland].

The letter went on to explain that although the surgery was easy, he had swelling and pain – "like a long, sharp, smooth ice pick" – and he was using heat packs and ointments to ease his discomfort. "It is best that I keep quiet, off my feet and avoid certain excitement," Snook wrote.

Chester watched the jury carefully, certain that none of the 11 male panelists could conceive of doing this type of surgery on themselves. The ladies in the stifling courtroom dabbed their fevered brows, their eyes wide with incredulous excitement.

After persistent questioning by Chester, Snook grudgingly admitted that he usually signed a woman's name to the letters – "Janet" was one he remembered using – but he signed "Mabel" to at least 11 of his letters introduced in court. Mabel was an interesting choice inasmuch as the secretary to Veterinary College Dean David S. White – and White's future second wife – was named Mabel. As Snook had said, "We used the name of women friends when we wrote." That brought laughter from some courtroom visitors.

Chester quickly changed the subject once again, trying to keep the defiant witness off-balance.

"Doctor, did Theora Hix ever express regret to you that she had ever started to have sexual intercourse with you?"

"I cannot just say that she expressed regret that she had started with me, but she expressed regret about starting and about keeping it up."

Chester began to read from another letter, but Ricketts objected. In fact, he entered an objection to the piecemeal reading of all the letters Chester possessed. Nevertheless, the Court allowed the prosecutor to proceed.

In another letter to Theora while she was in Cleveland, Snook wrote:

> My Dearie: Your morning note just received, and sorry you are so opposed and that is affecting your digestive department. I know exactly what you mean as I have been that way ever since you left except that two days in Cleveland. I am surprised to note that you put your entire condition of forlornness and turbulousness (sic) on the one thing and 'wish you never had.

Continuing the text of the letter, Chester noted the underlined words:

> <u>You once told me that you would never say that</u>. Neither do I believe it. You simply are alone and there, and that is new for you, especially in the past year, being alone, gives you time to think of the other. I could be contented just to be with you, omitting special features, and think you could also and I hope you will reconsider and can blame conditions rather than just the other [individual].

Students and department peers considered Snook a poor lecturer and a poorer speaker. His testimony, as well as the texts of letters, shows his lack of word power in the need to clearly express himself. He rambled and lacked clarity in sentence structure. Perhaps the vagueness was to mask their intimacies in case anyone ever found and read the letters. After one of Snook's visits to Cleveland, he wrote of his deeper feelings:

> My Dearie: Awakened early; about seven, and of course, thought of you at once. Wondered how tough it makes one feel for you to

awaken, turn over, reach before opening your eyes, and found <u>no one</u>. I know because I did it yesterday. 'Tis awful. Rustling through the papers last night and saw a funny that tickled me, and you can appreciate it. Quoting 'Button Buster' – I have heard it slightly different. It is told that they snap off (buttons) and put out the other fellow's eye. However they come from lower down and an entirely different cause, so beware if you are the cause, either stand very close or a little to one side.

In the 1920s the trouser fly was buttoned, not zipped.[24] Snook's humor is seen in this quip from a newspaper comic strip. Few saw the humor as Snook did, yet there was a ripple of laughter when Ricketts commented, "I suppose this goes in on the issue of insanity." Judge Scarlet guffawed. Mrs. Cassady stifled her giggle in her handkerchief.

Chester quizzed Snook on the times Theora refused to have sex with him. It had happened a few times, he admitted, but his letter gives a hint as to his surprise by her rejection:

I never had such a joke as when I closed the door, clicked the key and reached for you; a long trip, all anticipation, no chance soon again, and I was greeted with a "no, I don't want to muss my hair." and then, "I am hungry." Can you imagine anyone doing that? And further to sit quietly through a show for three hours more.

Snook had earlier testified that Meyers had loaned Theora his car while he was in Cleveland. She drove it while in school there, and she and Meyers supposedly returned in the car together after he had gone to pick her up. In another letter investigators found in Snook's office, Snook had other intentions:

You fix it up so that I can come up and drive home with you. If you can possibly keep the machine until then, it would be better than to

---

[24] The modern zipper was somewhat of a novelty in the 1920s, having been patented only in 1917.

jiggle down in the coupe. I know that you can miss one more class since you are so good in that work. However, you must write the instructor that you will be late and why. It sets them right so much better than an explanation afterward. If you don't know just who is to give the work, tell me the course numbers and I will find out. You can have a restful trip home, and that is what we both need, instead of your rushing down here pell-mell, be all tired out and have your room to fix up and all that. If I can see you at all, then it would have to be quick that Saturday afternoon and evening and Sunday or not until late in the week and that long a time would be awful.

Even then it would be the same old way, just part of a night and an afternoon. You would be too tired from all the hurry too. We must take advantage of opportunities to do something different, and this is one. Driving down, we could have two whole nights and a day all to ourselves and get in here Sunday in time for you to get things set fairly and then there would be no rush for you to arrange things.

Earlier, when the defense had questioned Snook, the innuendo had been that he was the victim of a possessive lover. For the benefit of his defense, he had portrayed himself as the passive fly, caught in Theora's web and unable to extricate himself because of her constant threats. The letters revealed him to be a decision-maker. He directed her as to procedures in cutting a class.

The letter also shows him as the aggressor, and so intense is his desire to see her that he rambles about his fears that they can't be together soon enough. He carefully had worked on the plan to get home and was anxious for them to take the trip from Cleveland to Columbus, which he planned would take two days and a night. In another letter, Chester read Snook's instructions to Theora about how to lie to Marion Meyers as to why she should drive to Columbus in his car – without Meyers. Snook told her to invent two girl students, who wanted her to drive them home and stop with them for a while:

Give one [of the girls] a home in Oberlin and one near Delaware.
Don't mention class on Saturday to him [Meyers].

By his own admission, in the past two years Snook rarely ate at home with his wife. Two or three times a week, at least, he picked up Theora about 5 p.m., drove to their love nest, and then about 8 p.m. they would go to dinner – The Clock on High Street and the Matsonia Barbecue on West Broad Street were favorite restaurant haunts. Helen Snook dined at home with the baby at 6 p.m.

It had become a most convenient arrangement for a husband engaged in an extramarital affair. Helen had access to charge accounts at three stores, and he gave her cash from $70 in monthly rent from the other half of the duplex (where her parents lived) and $25 from the occasional monthly rental to students of a third story room. He managed his annual tax-free salary of $4,000 ($48,000 in 2007 dollars), yet several times he complained to Theora that he was out of funds.

For the third time in the court session, there was a noisy disturbance from a "howling, whistling crowd" outside the courtroom, because they could neither get inside nor hear the trial proceedings. "We will have to clear the lobby if this demonstration is not stopped," an angry Judge Scarlett told his bailiffs. Several women "hiding" in the ladies room were rousted by Bailiff W. A. Craiglow, and the third-floor hallway was cleared temporarily until order was restored.

After the six weeks that Snook had promised Meyers he would have no contact with Theora, she phoned Snook and said it was all over with Meyers.

"She wanted to resume our relationship," said Snook. "He [Meyers] couldn't do for her what I could."

"What was that?" asked Chester.

"Well, sexual satisfaction."

"What?"

"Company, advice and talk."

"And what else?"

"And this money that I might fix for her so that she could go away. In other words, I had that. Her father had invested money in Florida and couldn't get it loose."

According to Snook, she would need the money to leave if they were ever "found out." If she wasn't going to resume her relationship with Snook at that time, she wouldn't need money for a quick getaway. To paint the dark picture for the jury, the prosecutor accused the witness of taking "advantage of a lonely, indigent girl."

Chester questioned the vet about the discrepancies in his stories about Theora's room key on June 13.

"Doctor, I will ask you if it is not a fact that you told Detective Phillips that you had had a discussion over the key; that she handed you the key; that you had handed the key back to her and that finally, when it ended up, that she had the key?"

"No sir, I did not."

"And doctor, on Thursday, June 20th, did you say to Chief French in his office at police headquarters, that you stopped at Scioto Country Club <u>after</u> you had murdered Theora Hix, in order to clean up before you came into town?"

"No, indeed, sir."

16 | IN THE COUPE

Prosecutor Chester had eagerly waited for this day in court. At the conclusion of his grueling cross-examination of Snook, he was confident that he would have the sharpshooter firmly planted in the electric chair.

Among courthouse veterans, however, the betting went to 3-to-1 in favor of Snook escaping Ohio's ultimate penalty.

In the courthouse Friday, the gallery of 300 sweltered. Before the day ended, a record nine women would faint from the oppressive heat in the courtroom and corridor outside. Nevertheless, most who experienced a touch of the vapors insisted on returning to their place in line or their seat in the gallery. Mrs. Catherine Green was not so fortunate, however. While she attended to a stranger who had fainted next to her, a thief made off with her purse.

The testimony this day – eight weeks after the discovery of Theora's lifeless body – focused on the sex between the professor and the coed just minutes before the murder. Once again the testimony was far too salacious for the newspapers to print, much to the dismay of avid readers. It led, however, to an enterprising yet short-lived bit of publishing titled *The Murder of Theora Hix*. At 35 cents apiece, copies of the pamphlet sold quickly, but only for 24 hours. The police raided downtown newsstands and confiscated all the copies they found, threatening to arrest those who peddled it.

From the outset it was clear that Chester took joy in asking the former professor for the smallest details as to "the manner in which you had sexual relations in the Ford coupe." A reporter for *The Ohio State Journal* observed that "the public is beginning to grow rather sallow around the gills after having too much of this rich diet, like one who indulges in bananas to excess." He predicted that after the trial "there will be a big need for a dose of mental castor oil to sort of purge the mind."

The prosecutor set the scene for the jury, putting Snook in the driver's seat and Theora beside him in the 1929 Ford coupe. "The pedals and the wheel and everything are on the left side of the car, aren't they?" The witness, appearing relaxed with his legs crossed and hands clasped in his lap, confirmed that they were. Those who were familiar with the model of the car and its small passenger compartment had a hard time envisioning any intimacy whatsoever in the coupe other than a hug and a kiss. Yet Snook, under Chester's blistering interrogation, described how Theora sat on the edge of the seat while he positioned his 6-foot, 190-pound frame down in front of her.

"And it was in that manner that you had sexual relations, was it?"

"Attempted to, yes, sir."

"Attempted to?"

In the courtroom, nervous giggles of embarrassment could not be held back. The judge coughed. None had difficulty imagining the act performed exactly as Snook described it.

"And in that position you were able to make connections with her?"

"Fairly so, but it was unsatisfactory."

"Fairly so?"

"Yes, sir."

"You were able to make an insertion were you, at that time?"

"Yes, sir."

Why did he not take the car blanket, get out of the car and have intercourse on the blanket on the ground, Chester wanted to know. It would have been easier for both, but Snook said they were "experimenting" with having sex for the first time in his new two-door coupe.

The spectators were finally getting what they came for. They, too, sat on the edges of their seats, absorbing images of the final encounter between the lovers.

"Did you have to squirm around and work a whole lot when you were trying to get in position there?" Chester asked, making the witness squirm.

"Naturally, in the machine."

"Was the right door on the coupe open or closed?"

"Open."

"It was open. Where were your feet, doctor?"

"Well, I don't know as to that."

"Were they out of the door or were they inside of the coupe?"

"One of them would be out; one of them had to be out."

"Well, now, was it out or was it in?"

"It was in," Snook recalled, but Chester pushed the issue to ridiculousness – becoming a hokeypokey inquiry: left foot in, right foot out. Finally the prosecutor moved on.

"Doctor, what became of Theora Hix's legs at that time? Did they go down through the floor or what happened to them?"

"They were elevated, to the best of my knowledge."

"Elevated to what or where?" Chester continued, enjoying the discomfort he was causing his witness. Snook pulled out a paper fan to stir the warm, still air and maintain his cool.

"Simply held up," he replied.

"They were simply held up?"

"Yes, sir."

"She held her legs up in the air?"

"Yes, sir."

"I see. All the time that you had intercourse with her?"

"Well, partly."

"Partly? Did she put them down at any time?"

"Well," Snook said, "she moved them around, couldn't put them down. That was what made it unsatisfactory."

Whatever tragic images had been envisioned as to the terrible moments leading up to Theora's death, the victim's posthumous dignity would suffer from Snook's testimony of their last moments together, engaged in awkward sex.

Theora had an orgasm, Snook believed, but he did not, electing to withdraw early "before there was any trouble started." It was another strange admission, given that earlier he had told the Court that he'd given himself a partial vasectomy, which would have made him sterile.

The lovers returned to their original positions, straightening out their disheveled clothes in the process. After buttoning his fly, Snook sat back in the driver's seat, preparing to drive off. He turned the key on the right side of the small dashboard to start the engine, but she stopped him. "'We are not going now,'" he recalled her saying. In no uncertain terms, she told him that he was not going to visit his mother over the Father's Day weekend in Lebanon, as he had planned, he said. Weekends were to be her time, she declared. It was an argument that they had had before.

Before continuing his relentless line of questioning, Chester held up various undergarments Theora wore and asked the witness to describe how each silky garment fastened. Another distasteful and embarrassing experience for Snook.

"Then, doctor, what was the next move she made?"

"She grabbed for me and started to go down, holding the buttons open and unbuttoned my trousers."

Chester pressed the interrogation, knowing that he had the entire courtroom wrapped around his every word. In the jury box, Mrs. Cassady lowered her gaze to the floor in an attempt to hide her flushed face behind the wide-brim of her hat.

"What movements did she make now, doctor? Tell us in detail just what she did."

"She pulled my right leg over, pulled them apart, and then down on her knees, went right down that way with her head."

The prosecutor wanted to know in what "condition" Snook found himself: "erect or soft?" He answered in the negative: "It was not erect, no."

"Did she open your trousers?"

"She did."

"All the way?"

"Clear up to the belt."

Chester turned to face the jury. "And then did she reach in after your penis?" he asked with derision.

"She did."

The jury sat stunned. Many blushed, as did Snook. The gallery was as quiet as anytime during the trial. Mouths dropped open, as if to hear better.

In response to questions, Snook described how the young woman got down on her knees, pulling his hips toward her. Then she proceeded "to go down" on him: Snook did not resist. He had allowed her to do that in previous encounters. "She proceeded to help herself," he said, "and I didn't do anything just then." But then, he said, "she got rough about it."

Snook admitted she bit his flaccid penis several times, "but she bit too hard right at the beginning. She continued to bite."

"Did she make any scars on you?" asked Chester.

"Well, not particularly scars that I know of, but it was enough to bruise it and hurt."

"Was there any blood there, doctor?"

"No, sir."

The prosecutor was in full cry now, chasing down the accused. "Then, after she bit you, then what did she do, doctor?"

"Well, when she first started to bite me [she] reached in with her hand and took hold of the scrotum."

"She took hold of the scrotum? What did she do with it after she took hold of it?"

"She pulled and kept on biting, doing her best to help herself, the way she had done before."

"Had she done that same thing before, doctor? She had bit you before?"

"No, I mean getting hold of it and moving it up and down ... moving her mouth up and down on the penis."

"I see. Then did that hurt, doctor?"

Snook adamantly responded, "Yes, indeed," but he appeared unruffled.

It was easy to imagine that every male in the courtroom felt the pain. Mrs. Cassady and others hid their embarrassment in their hands.

Snook said he attempted to push Theora's head away, but she only held on harder "and that made it hurt worse."

"That made it hurt worse?"

"Yes, then I reached underneath and tried to choke her... [but] I couldn't get ahold to choke her and then I pulled her head in closer. The closer in I pulled it, the easier it seemed to be."

"Let's see," said Chester. "You said you couldn't get ahold of her to choke her?"

"Yes."

"Why, doctor?"

"She was right down here between my knees," Snook said.

Snook said he tried to twist away from his paramour, in doing so kicking violently. He continued to hold her head close to relieve his pain and "telling her to quit... to stop, but she didn't do it, and she kept on pulling and then she pulled hard on the scrotum."

At this point, the defendant said, he "reached up for the hammer and hit her with it." The initial blow to the head forced Theora to let go.

"Then I grabbed her wrist and twisted it – twisted her back onto the seat."

Chester wanted a demonstration and took up a position on his knees next to the seated witness to replicate the struggle. "Go ahead and push me," he said. "Take that wrist and take me out over... go on, push me right up like that."

Snook did his best but Chester demanded more physical exertion. "Just throw me right around," he said. "You needn't worry about me.

You could not hurt me... Go on." Snook grabbed the prosecutor's left wrist and twisted it so hard that Chester almost went over a table.

After getting Theora back on the seat by forcefully twisting her arm, the witness said she reached behind the seat to get her purse, screaming: 'Damn you! I will kill you now!"

Chester wanted to make sure the jury had an accurate picture of what actually happened in the front seat of the car. He placed two chairs side-by-side immediately in front of the jury box. He told Snook to be seated on the "driver's side" while he sat in what would have been the victim's position. The prosecutor then directed Snook to explain what happened next.

Theora slid off the seat and slipped out of the car, he said.

"Slid right off the seat, kind of like that?" Chester asked, athletically slipping off his chair until he nearly fell on the floor.

"I grabbed for her and pulled her back onto the seat," Snook said. The two men went through the gyrations of re-creating the act.

"What became of the hammer?" the prosecutor wanted to know.

"I had ahold of it or it was right on the seat."

As Theora and Snook struggled, he repeatedly hit her with the hammer and tried to retrieve the purse, which he believed contained a pistol. Then they both fell out of the car. Finally, a mighty blow to the side of her head.

Tears came to Snook's eyes.

"This was when she fell, then the door went shut, and she fell so she hit the running board of the machine. She rolled over and over away from the machine."

"And that is all? You don't know what you did from that time on?"

"No, I don't. I know that I doubled up and was sitting on the running board of the machine, holding my scrotum with both hands." Repeatedly he said he could not remember how many times he hit Theora with the hammer, which he now used to lightly tap the kneecap of his crossed leg while testifying.

Nor could he remember telling investigators that he cut Theora's jugular vein with a pocketknife, as Chester put it, "to make her death easy."

"You don't remember telling us that?"

"Well, I didn't tell you that because I didn't remember it." It was one of dozens of times during the cross-examination that Snook failed to recall the incident as described by the prosecutor.

"And if we say that you did say that, we are liars, aren't we?" the prosecutor shouted.

"Yes, sir," the confident witness replied with a wry smile.

Snook described for the court the various bruises to his arm and leg, the bite on the penis, and a hand still sore after hurting it the day before the murder.

"After you were sitting on the running board, what did you say to her at that time, doctor?"

"Oh, I just called to her; I can't tell what words I said, but I just said, 'Come on, let's go.'"

"Did you call her by name?"

"No, I never did call her by name."

"But you are positive you did call her?"

"I said something to her, but she didn't move ... Then I realized then that somebody might come in there – we might be seen or something of that kind – and I got up and looked around." Snook said he "clambered" back in the coupe and drove away.

"Why did you leave, doctor, without knowing what her condition was?"

"Well, I was scared. I was afraid someone would come in there."

"Scared of your shadow?"

"Yes."

Chester now shouted his questions: "You knew the girl was lying there in the weeds, didn't you, doctor?"

"Yes, sir."

"And yet, you drove away not knowing if she was dead or alive?"

"Well, I spoke to her, and she didn't move or didn't answer."

"So that you knew that she was dead, didn't you, doctor?"

"Yes, sir."

According to Chester, Snook jumped in his car and drove away as quickly as possible, telling police later that 'I was a damned coward, because I got away from there as fast as I could.'" Again the defendant denied Chester's version of events.

"How long after the murder occurred on the range, before the pain (on the penis) eased up?" Snook was asked.

"Oh, I don't know just how long, but I knew it was better after I got into the machine – but it didn't hurt intensely because I got out to get a newspaper, because I remember walking across the street fairly good."

"You were able to think about getting a paper?"

"I always get a paper at about 9:30."

Chester turned to what he believed to be the many conflicting statements of the accused.

"Had not you told Chief French you had not seen Theora Hix after June 11th?"

"No, sir."

"Didn't Chief French relate to you the circumstances on June 13th and said: 'Doctor, on the night that Theora Hix started over to the University Hospital, shortly after she left the apartment, one of the Bustin girls observed that she had forgotten her keys and had picked them up off the furniture upon which they were lying and made the remark to her sister who was present, saying that Theora had forgotten her keys, and one of them would have to stay there until she came back; and that she [Alice Bustin] examined them, that she observed a strange key on the ring, that she had not seen there before, and then, they were discussing the fact that one would remain home so that Theora could get in. Theora came running up the steps and into the room and said that she had forgotten her keys and just jerked them out of [Alice Bustin's] hand and put them in her purse and started back [out] again?'"

"I never heard that statement before," Snook said, once again having a memory lapse. Repeatedly, he denied having given details as described by the prosecution. In fact, at the time of his arrest, Snook initially denied ever having been with Theora on the night of the murder. He saw her last on Monday, June 10, he said.

Chester continued to press for straight answers: "And later, after further interrogation [at police headquarters], at along 6 o'clock in the morning, didn't you tell the chief you had enjoyed the whole procedure up to that point and ... that you wanted to see one of your attorneys?"

"Positively not. I simply didn't enjoy it, so that I know I didn't say that."

Chester brought up a statement that had been made earlier by Detective Phillips.

"Doctor, there are hundreds of people who know where the New York [Central] rifle range is located. There are always a number of people who know who Theora Hix is, but that you are the only man that the police could find who knew Theora Hix, and also knew where the rifle range was located."

Sexual perversion was another line of Chester's paced questioning, turning, pausing and pointing to the prisoner. "All right. Now, doctor ...why didn't you, at the time that you had the marks upon you, tell the proper authorities what happened out there at the rifle range?"

"I didn't tell anybody; I didn't tell the attorneys or anybody, simply because I was ashamed of it."

"You were ashamed of it?"

"Yes, indeed, I was."

"Ashamed of the whole shooting match, weren't you?" The young prosecutor smiled at his choice of words.

"Ashamed of any sex perversion, because I never knew anyone that would do that before."

Chester faced the jury and shouted once again, "You could commit murder, but you were ashamed of showing the marks on your body?"

Ricketts popped up from his chair, "I object!" he shouted.

"I didn't admit it," said Snook.

"Didn't admit what?" Chester shouted.

"Didn't admit murder."

"Don't you admit it now?"

"No, he doesn't and never has!" Ricketts roared anew, jumping out of his seat. He wanted no mention made of premeditated murder, or murder in the first degree, the penalty for which was death in the electric chair.

Judge Scarlett overruled the objection. Snook said he was not admitting to murder, a word the defense avoided.

"Did you kill the girl?"

"I told you that I did because she threatened my wife and baby and then threatened to to kill me," Snook replied. "That is the only statement I made to you at the time of the confession."

Smelling blood, Chester refused to let the witness off the hook. "Well, now, you do admit that you killed her, don't you?"

Ricketts' objection was overruled by the Court. Snook repeated his statement that he felt threatened by Theora.

"Now, do I understand that you don't admit to killing?"

"I admit that I killed the girl to protect my wife and baby and then she threatened me." Chester had what he wanted the jury to hear.

Finally, a somewhat harried Snook stepped down after 17 hours on the stand over three days. During the recess, he told reporters that when he had the hammer in his hand to demonstrate the blows for Chester, "I could have got (sic) even with him for those socks in the head he gave me with his fist over at police headquarters. ... One blow with that hammer could have made up for several of the kind he gave me."

17 | THE SLAP

J ohn J. Chester Jr. turned 31 on Saturday, August 10.

Theora K. Hix would have turned 25 the same day.

Sitting in Chester's second-floor office, as he had done throughout the trial, Dr. Melvin Hix held his head in his hands. As he thought about his only child on this special day, tears streamed down his cheeks. When Theora was home, her parents always had a birthday cake for her.

Hix accused Snook of painting "a picture that nobody else can connect with that girl (Theora). ... Those are all lies, I am sure."

Mrs. Hix had been constantly at her husband's side, waiting for news of the trial and reading newspaper accounts, but she could not bring herself to accompany her husband to the courthouse this day.

Interest in the trial waned somewhat on Saturday, now that Snook had had his say, but Mrs. Margaret Farley was happy. The proprietor of the courthouse lunch stand reported record sales during Snook's testimony. Before breakfast Saturday morning,, members of the jury members of the jury participated in some exercise. Under the watchful eye of bailiffs, the group hiked from the Southern Hotel to Parsons Avenue and back, about a two-mile jaunt.

When the doors opened to the courtroom at 9 a.m. Saturday, standing room for about 50 more was available. Edward Clark once again secured a front-row seat, keeping his perfect attendance record alive.

Harry F. Busey, in a column on the editorial page of *The Columbus Citizen* Saturday, noted that the "Snook trial has given Columbus the expected dirt bath. ... Even the unprintable portions of his testimony are common talk. Just how good or bad this is for the community, we can't judge, but certainly there is no urge to go do likewise."

He also reported, with tongue in cheek, that sales of love nests in the metropolitan area had reached "epidemic" proportions. "Evidently some folks are heeding a danger signal, temporarily at least."

Several witnesses – a cabinetmaker and a sporting-goods salesman, for instance – took the stand to testify as to the good character of the defendant and admit that he was known to be a "peaceable and quiet" fellow. Some witnesses had donated funds for Snook's defense, although the names of donors remained anonymous.

Also taking the stand Saturday morning was Robert W. Terry, who identified himself as a pharmacist, chemist and bacteriologist. To the amusement of the jury, he arrived with mortar and pestle and a batch of green blister beetles, otherwise known as Spanish fly. He skillfully ground them up into a powder that was passed among the panel so each could examine it under a magnifying glass. Shiny flecks of green from the beetle's outer shell were visible.

By putting Terry on the stand, the defense hoped to discredit the testimony of the State's chemist C.F. Long, who testified to having found aphrodisiacs in Theora's stomach but saw no green flecks. Under standard testing, Terry maintained, such specks indicated a presence of Spanish fly. But then, Long's reputation as a chemist was "not so good," the witness said.

Dr. Frank W. Harrah, an urologist, testified as to the "wounds" Snook suffered in the coupe. Twice he had examined Snook's genitals for bruising and "indentations." Unfortunately, with just a word or two, Harrah all but stripped away the last vestiges of Snook's manhood. He divulged what no man wants to hear about himself, especially in the company of more than 200 strangers in the courtroom.

"The penis is rather small in size," the physician began, reading from his examination notes. A ripple of giggles came from the gallery. Mrs. Cassady stared at her hands in her lap. Snook slumped farther into his chair as Harrah described small irregularities, slight discolorations and a few indentations. A small scar from the vasectomy was evident, the physician said.

Chester cross-examined: "If you bruised your eye and bruised the penis with about the same force, they would clear up about the same length of time?"

"I judge so," said Dr. Harrah.

In an unusual move, Seyfert called to the witness stand his associates, first Seidel and then Ricketts. The defense wanted the jury to hear about purported irregularities by police and the prosecutors that led to Snook's arrest and "alleged confession" after the slapping incident.

Former Municipal Court Judge Seidel was first up. He spoke of meeting with Snook at police headquarters the Saturday after the murder, then being at the Snook home while police searched it. When Seyfert picked out from the exhibits a compact taken from Snook's furnace, Seidel said he could not identify it because investigators had not properly identified it. Chester objected to the response.

"If the Court will please instruct Judge Seidel that he is on the stand, just ordinary witness, and that he must not make speeches on that stand."

"Never mind," Judge Scarlett responded, allowing his former colleague some latitude.

According to the witness, the following Monday both he and Ricketts tried to see their client but they were "flatly refused" unless Chester gave his approval. That's when the defense team secured a mandatory injunction from Judge Dana Reynolds.

"I was in three homicide cases against Mr. Chester, and I knew his tactics. I knew that he didn't play square where his own publicity was involved, and I told Ricketts, 'Don't fool with that pup; he absolutely won't keep his word,'" Seidel testified.

After the all-night grilling of the accused, Seidel said that Chester told him at the county jail that "'this fellow is about to confess, and he wants to talk to you.'" But the attorney said emphatically that Snook had not confessed to anything, a fact Seidel soon relayed to Chester.

According to the witness, Chester said: "'John Seidel, damn you. If you don't have that fellow confess, I am going to ruin you,'" Seidel recalled. "'I am going to give it to the other papers right this minute!'"

"I will be damned if you will ruin me," Seidel said he responded angrily. "I will not make any man confess."

Finally, cooler heads prevailed, and Seidel said he was permitted to sit in on the questioning of his client – providing that he follow Chester's rules and remain silent. However, two or three times Seidel interrupted Chester's interrogation, at one point telling his client to "tell him what you told me." An angry prosecutor had had enough, saying:

> John Seidel, you shut up! You get your hat and coat and get right out of here. ... You get out before you get thrown out!

Seidel said the door slammed behind him, and "I heard considerable commotion in the room, like two men scuffling." To a group of newspaper reporters standing around in the hall, Seidel described Chester as "the god-damnedest, most unethical dog I ever saw!"

The next time Seidel said he saw Snook, he noticed "a big red spot on his right cheek ... and I noticed one on the right, close to the ear, and one on the left, marks that remained for two or three days."

At this point Judge Scarlett adjourned the trial until Monday morning, when Chester's cross-examination of Seidel began. Although witness and prosecutor quibbled and squabbled over many little details, Seidel's story remained much the same. Then Chester caught him with a question out of left field.

"I will ask you if you didn't tell the newspapermen at that time that now famous remark of yours, 'If Snook killed the girl, I helped him do it'?" It was a comment widely published, but Seidel denied Chester's version. He said his utterance came after Snook swore to him on a handshake that he did not "murder" Theora.

"I have changed my mind, after he told me with his own lips that he took the girl's life, but I told him that he wasn't guilty of murder," Judge Seidel said.

During Chester's cross-examination, Seidel made it clear that he did not learn from Snook about the "perversion" in the coupe until Monday, August 2, or almost two months after the murder. Obviously, the accused had not been as forthcoming with his attorneys as one might have expected.

At the conclusion of his cross-examination, Chester asked Seidel: "Evidently no love lost between you and myself, is there, judge?"

"No, Jack, you are a wonderful fellow, but you have got your faults and so have I."

Ricketts had his own way of testifying: "I would rather say what I have to say here without any questions." He rambled on almost uninterrupted about the arrest and interrogation of his client, whom he found to be "absolutely incoherent in his answers ... repeating over and over again what [Detective] Phillips had said that he had done." Ricketts also noted marks on his client's cheeks, "as if he had been hit with the flat of a hand on either side."

The week had seen a hard-fought battle between attorneys, taxing all involved. The weekend brought a welcome rest. Saturday and Sunday afternoons, the jury panel attended baseball games between Columbus and Milwaukee at Neil Park.

18 | 'NEVER BURN'

"**S**nook will never burn!"

The animated Ricketts expressed his conviction to James L. Kilgallen of International News Service that even if the jury found his client guilty of first-degree murder without mercy, mandating the death penalty, "there are enough reversible errors in the case to save him from such a fate."

The defense attorney exuded confidence. "We have contended that Snook was insane when the crime was committed, and I am sure that the jury has long since arrived at this conclusion."

Somewhat surprisingly, the defense abruptly rested its case at 2:35 p.m. Monday, August 13, two months to the day after Theora's death. Counsel had been expected to call several alienists to support the insanity theory, but Ricketts decided it would not be necessary to do so.

The prosecution called a half-dozen rebuttal witnesses to the stand, including Detective Phillips, to reinforce the State's key points. For instance, Phillips said Snook told him two days after the killing that he thought some degenerate had killed Theora in an effort to place the blame elsewhere. The officer also quoted the professor as having said, "If I killed her, I was sane." If true, the utterance would knock a hole in the insanity defense, but Snook denied ever having said anything of the kind.

After numerous acrimonious clashes between opposing attorneys, Phillips testified what the one-time suspect Marion Meyers had told him: that Theora had said she would kill Snook if he had given her a venereal disease. Her tests came back negative, however.

Police stenographer Ralph O. Brown also took the stand as a rebuttal witness. Guided by a watery-eyed, sniffling Chester – he suffered from hay fever – Brown read his notes from the "alleged confession," quoting Snook as having admitted that he had "fractured" Theora's skull "and to relieve her suffering, I severed her jugular vein with my pocketknife." Snook could not remember ever having said or done that. Nevertheless, his signature appeared on Brown's stenopad, which the prosecution finally introduced as evidence.

When Chief Harry E. French became a rebuttal witness for the State, more bitter banter ensued. A particularly lively debate concerned the white-haired chief's recollection of the slaps Chester dealt Snook. Finally, French, who proved to be a worthy adversary for Ricketts on cross-examination, told what he remembered of the incident.

"I sat looking out [the window] towards Fulton Street and just about that time I heard a sound of that sort," slapping his hands together loudly. "I turned instantly and when I did…I saw Mr. Chester's [left] hand hit him…and immediately after that with the right hand, flat. I observed Dr. Snook's glasses come off his face and fell (sic) at his feet on the floor." French said he heard one blow and saw two. "I think that Mr. Chester's feelings got a little [the] better of him, but he apologized."

As Ricketts started to object, Assistant Prosecutor Hicks stopped him, and Chester jumped in, too. "Never mind your remarks," he told Ricketts. "Nobody wants to hear them."

"I don't care whether you do or not, I am not talking to you!" Ricketts shouted. Judge Scarlett called a halt to the verbal battle and shortly thereafter adjourned the Monday afternoon session for the day.

On the stand again Tuesday morning, Chief French clarified for the jury that Chester's slap with an open hand did not break Snook's glasses. He described the defendant as "the most self-possessed man that I have ever helped to interrogate in 29 years." During his long interrogation, French said Snook maintained "an amused, sneering sort of smile on his face, rocked himself backwards and forwards on [the rear legs of] his chair and seemed to be enjoying himself quite thoroughly, never ruffled in the least. Nothing that was said to him seemed to stir him out of his habitual calm." On the other hand, when Snook did shed tears, French believed the cause to be "the pricking of a guilty conscience."

Throughout the questioning of the chief, Ricketts continued his running verbal battle with Chester and his associates – and with the witness on occasion. When the phrase *legal verbiage* came up, Ricketts asked French, "Are you a lawyer?"

"No, I am proud to say I am not, Mr. Ricketts." Spectators snickered.

"I don't blame you. I want to congratulate you on your feeling about the matter."

"It is bad enough to be a policeman," the ruddy-faced officer stated, much to the amusement of the spectators. Judge Scarlett wielded his gavel to quiet the guffaws.

Ricketts also used the phrase, *third degree*, to which French replied: "I have heard of the third degree. I have seen it depicted in the movies. I've read about it in fiction books, but I have never known of such a thing…in the police headquarters of this city."

Chief French recalled a conversation he had with Snook at the conclusion of the inquisition. According to the witness, the defendant laughed and described the questioning by the law officers as "the most humorous and ridiculous thing that I have ever seen. Why, these fellows are very crude. They will never get anything on me at all."

The irony was, of course, that the prosecutors and lawmen did get something: a confession (several versions, in fact), significant physical evidence and a grand jury indictment. Whether a conviction would follow remained to be seen.

Judge Scarlett excused the jury while the defense argued for a directed verdict "for the reason that the State has failed to prove the manner and means of death as laid in the indictment." Even the coroner, Dr. Murphy, admitted that death *might* have ensued as a result of some other injury not cited in the indictment, Ricketts argued.

Once again, when Ricketts made a reference to "the law," he squared off with Chester.

"What is the law?" Chester asked stridently. "I haven't heard any law yet. I have heard a lot of argument but no law."

"You wouldn't recognize it if you would hear it."

"Probably not. Coming from your lips I couldn't even hear it."

"No, I appreciate that," said Ricketts. "Any juvenile outburst won't affect this case."

"No. Neither will any senile outburst affect this case," Chester responded.

Scarlett halted the bickering by giving his observations on "the law." He called it "unfortunate" that the indictment included but one means of death. "I think the better plan would have been to plead them both" – from hammer blows and from a cut jugular vein. In the end, however, he overruled the defense motion. He ruled likewise against the defense motion to withdraw the charge of first-degree murder.

Tuesday afternoon Mrs. Helen Chapman, her arm in a sling, found a seat in the spectators' section. The previous week a surging crowd of spectators pushed her down, and she broke her arm.

Assistant Prosecuting Attorney Paul C. Hicks led off closing arguments for the State, followed by E.O. Ricketts for the defense. Wednesday's lineup featured Max C. Seyfert for the defense, followed by Assistant Prosecutor Myron B. Gessaman, defense attorney John F. Seidel, and, batting cleanup for Ohio, the 31-year-old "boy prosecutor" John J. Chester Jr. Each attorney had an hour.

For him, Hicks told the jury panel, it was "a very plain case of murder in the first degree." After severing Theora's jugular vein with a pocketknife, beating her about the head at least a dozen times with a hammer and covering up practically every detail imaginable of his crime, "this defendant's past reputation as to being peaceable and quiet avails him absolutely nothing and should be disregarded."

Even though Snook felt threatened by a pistol he believed to be in Theora's purse, Hicks noted that the pistol was found in her dressing table drawer, in a box and underneath some stockings.

"You are asked to believe tommyrot," he told the jurors. "Things like that don't happen, except in this defendant's imagination, and he has got it working overtime, just like a machine gun."

"If he killed Miss Hix in self-defense, why would he repeatedly tell falsehoods to the police authorities… and even lie to his own attorneys?"

Hicks questioned the professor's fitness as a husband and father. "I just wonder how many times he has been at home with his wife around the dinner hour to partake of a meal with her at the table, and how many times he had this little baby, their little girl, in his arms?"

After the killing at the rifle range, Snook "went home, put his car in the garage, went to a drugstore, bought a *Night Green* [newspaper edition], came home, went out in the kitchen, cooked some hamburger, fixed himself a lunch [snack] and ate it, read the front page of the *Green* and then went to bed and slept all night [while Theora] was out there on the rifle range, face down, with the rain falling on her back."

"If there was ever a case presented to a jury in this county where the extreme penalty should be imposed, this is absolutely one."

Ricketts, who limited his rambling summation somewhat because he admitted to feeling poorly, initially focused on the manner in which the prosecution obtained "this alleged confession" from Snook. "Mr. Chester hasn't any more right to slap the face of this man once, twice or three times than this man had, as a matter of law, to kill this woman," he said. He also pointed out that Chester denied Snook counsel during questioning and threatened to ruin the career of co-counsel, Seidel. Such acts Ricketts found "reprehensible."

In addition, he said that the State had failed to present "a single scintilla of evidence as to the motive… as to the design and purpose of this act," defense counsel stated, "and they have not shown premeditation." That made it a case of second-degree murder at most, he said, fighting to keep his client out of the electric chair.

Ricketts laced his remarks with invectives against the State. He riled Chester once again when he suggested the prosecution sought to make "political hay" by charging a prominent member of the Ohio State faculty with first-degree murder.

"Wait a minute!" Chester yelled, rising from his chair. "Are they going to argue politics in the case?" Judge Scarlett allowed the defense to continue, which Ricketts did with a lengthy explanation of murder in the first degree versus in the second degree. It was pretty dry stuff for the jurors.

He next impeached Theora's character as someone who had "dominated" Snook. "She would not let him go down and visit his old mother, the old lady here, 70-odd-years old!" His client also felt threatened by the coed, who possessed a pistol and knew how to shoot it. "Yes, she could shoot," Ricketts reminded the jury, "and she could shoot straight!"

After describing the former professor's embarrassment at having engaged in "an unnatural sexual act" which all but maimed Snook, Ricketts' summation suddenly came to an end when Judge Scarlett called an adjournment for the day. It was Ricketts' last hurrah.

The 18th and final day of the trial got off to a halting start Wednesday morning. Before the four concluding arguments could begin, Judge Scarlett announced that one of the jurors, namely C.F. Butche, had been "seized with an old-fashioned bilious[25] attack" overnight. The Southern Hotel physician, Dr. Olin R. Martin, examined the stricken juror and told Judge Scarlett that Butche could not continue on the panel.

---

[25] An excessive secretion of bile.

"I guess the inactivity of sitting in the jury seat for three weeks, coupled with the mental strain and high tension in the courtroom, was too much for me," said Butche, a carpenter by trade.

By agreement, the alternate, Newton L. Tracy, was seated in his stead, and the trial continued without a new alternate.

Siefert stood before the jury to argue for the defense. He described Theora as a "sneaky," mysterious individual who never went to church, who often came and went without saying a word to her roommates.

"The prosecution will try to... to make it appear that Snook dragged down this girl's morale along the gutter or plunged her soul – if she had one – to the depths of hell.""It was their duty, he told the jurors, "to drag this Hix girl out, naked as the day she was born, whether she was filthy with sin, whether she was a drug addict or whether she was an immoral person; those facts have to be disclosed."

Siefert ripped Coroner Murphy's autopsy as "absolutely pathetic in every respect." Theora died "as a result of the biggest thing that can cause death, and you write it, my friends, in three letters: S-I-N."

During Chester's lengthy so-called inquisition at police headquarters, Snook was "at the mercy of the wolves of the prosecutor's office," Siefert said. The interrogators would have continued "until they made that man a babbling idiot."

Hix knew that once she had Snook's handwritten letters in her possession, she had "him in the palm of her hand," according to the defense attorney. "She knew ... the publication ... of the letters in her possession would spell not only ruination for him as far as the university was concerned, it would tear apart his wife and himself, it would absolutely disgrace him and absolutely would cast him out of any and all good society. She knew he would be ostracized from even the ordinary social festivities, instead of enjoying the high esteem which he enjoyed up to that time."

The prosecution painted an entirely different picture of Theora. She was, Gessaman said, "a retiring, modest, capable girl, leading a clean, moral life." Pointing his finger at the sullen Snook, the attorney maintained that "if she was a sex pervert, you made her that!" As a full professor, the defendant held himself up as an example to the students of the university and yet "you led this girl into a life of immorality!" Again almost in the now-reddened face of the veterinarian, Gessaman shouted, "You accuse her of being a sex pervert and now you come before the jury here, parade your mother and your wife and your child that you never cared anything for and ask for mercy at the hands of this jury!"

Gessaman's description of the murder contradicted the version that Snook told. Snook severed the victim's jugular vein and carotid artery with the "cool hand" of a surgeon, he said, "then proceeded to pound her on the back of the head ... and drove her skull into her brain." The severe beating with a hammer was an effort to make everyone believe that a degenerate had executed Theora, "not a man who is well-educated, with the high standing of Dr. Snook."

He asked the jury to remember just how "cool" Snook was as a witness – "as cool as an iceberg. He was handed a cup of water by [former] Judge Seidel on that witness stand, not a quiver in the hand that took that cup of water, and there wasn't a quiver in that hand on the night of June 13, when he cut the jugular vein and carotid artery of Theora Hix."

A very tired Seidel spoke the final words for the defense, turning to the Bible to "find the frailty of human nature" and quoting from the Scriptures. In a voice that shook with emotion, he railed against the police investigation and the autopsy, but surprisingly saved his sharpest words for his client.

Snook was "the dumbest man that I ever represented in my life," he said. Some jurors seemed taken aback. If Seidel wanted to shock them, he succeeded. He described his client's behavior as "the acts of a child. Why, an ordinary Flytown[26] colored man committing a crime would throw the hammer away. He would throw the knife away. He would hide things. He would have taken the cleaning fluid from the back of his

---

[26] A Columbus neighborhood in decline.

car; he would not have left any gloves there; he would not have left any cap there – not a thing to discover his connection with it [the murder]."

Seidel described as "the most ridiculous thing in the world" the notion that Theora needed aphrodisiacs – allegedly provided by her lover – to stir her passion. "A man at 48 [Snook] in my judgment is going downhill pretty fast. He needs the pep. But the 24-year-old girl, she does not need any. She, as a woman, has more [sex drive] and … can always satisfy more than one man if she is bad." By "bad," Seidel implied Theora was a prostitute.

He pictured Snook as "a poor simp" who, after being repeatedly hounded and threatened by Theora, should have taken his fist and knocked her "into the middle of next week."

Seidel expressed pity for Snook, facing having to "go down life's pathway alone" and in disgrace, but he only had scorn for Theora, who, "in her madness and her drug addictiveness … would have shot them [Helen Snook and her daughter] down in cold blood." Snook acted because he believed his life was in danger, the attorney said in his final plea to the jurors, "and if he was, you should have the moral courage to say so and to free him."

"A maudlin crowd of thrill-crazed spectators" packed the courtroom after the recess for lunch, watched over by 18 deputies posted to maintain order. More than 500 spectators stuffed into a over heated room with a capacity to seat 200. Outside the courtroom, individuals stood on chairs on the chance they could see or hear the young prosecutor's final argument, anticipating that it would be something special. He did not disappoint, but he started slowly, citing Ohio law in some detail. Then he got down to the crime for which Snook was on trial.

Key to Chester's argument was the manner in which Theora was slain – from a knife wound to the throat, as stated in the indictment. In his testimony Snook could not remember that part, the prosecutor said, because if he did, it would show premeditation. Chester introduced a bit of drama to prove his point. He had Franklin County Detective Howard Lavely lie on the floor in front of the jury to play the victim.

After taking several blows to the head, Theora fell out of the car and onto her back, Chester said, swinging the hammer in evidence. Then, kneeling behind Lavely's head, the prosecutor demonstrated how Snook opened up his pocketknife, put on a pair of gloves and "stuck the knife in her ear – as he [Snook] says, to lessen her pain." Lifting Lavely's head and shoulders slightly, the athletic prosecutor demonstrated how Snook reached around the young woman's neck and put "a 4 ½-inch cut right there in her throat," using the knife to point to the area of the jugular vein. According to the State's scenario, Snook then rolled Theora over on her face, came down with the hammer, put at least a dozen wounds in the back of her head and pounded her face down into mud and weeds.

Snook "reverted to type," Chester said, pointing out that veterinarians killed animals by striking them in the head first, then cutting the throat. "That's what happened here. ... He hit her in the head and then bled her to death."

With Lavely now rolled over on his stomach, Chester invited jurors to step outside the jury box and take a look for themselves, as if they were looking at Theora's lifeless body. Only Wilby L. Balthaser, an elderly grocer and confectioner, did so. Slowly he walked all the way around the prone detective, stooped at one point for a closer look, nodded his approval and resumed his seat. It was stunning courtroom drama.

According to Snook, he went to the rifle range to have intercourse – "a despicable story," Chester continued. If true, he asked, why did the defendant not take his blanket on the nice warm night and lay it out in the field? Instead, the professor chose to have intercourse in his automobile – "in a Ford coupe! Now, believe that if you can!"

Why didn't Snook take more care to cover up his crime, the prosecutor asked? "Look at him there," Chester said, pointing to the defendant, slumped in his chair. "He is so darned egotistical that he thought he was a little bit smarter than anybody else. That is why he didn't cover it up. He is smart up at the university when it comes to cutting a horse or something of that kind, but when he came down to the police department, he forgot that he was playing the other fellow's game."

Mrs. Bertha Smith, a spectator standing in the enclosure for visiting attorneys, briefly interrupted Chester's argument: She fainted. Several persons revived her in an anteroom occupied by Helen Snook and her mother-in-law. Both covered their faces during the incident, not wishing to be recognized.

Snook washed the blood off his pocketknife and hammer and put them away and had his suit cleaned because "he is tight," Chester asserted, racing along like a 12-cylinder Ferrari. "He didn't like to spend his money. If he had thrown the suit away, it would have cost him $22 more. Or if he had thrown the hammer away, it would have cost him 55 cents. If he had thrown the penknife away, that would have cost him something, too." As a full professor, Snook had money, Chester noted, as well as a house, a new automobile and enough money to spend on Theora "to turn her head."

More drama ensued as Chester picked up from the exhibit table Theora's pink silk chemise, bloodstained and disheveled. "It is the most modest garment that there is, and it tells the story of that girl," he said, holding it high so all could see. He pointed out where "the little suit of underwear" was cut by Snook to facilitate intercourse with the victim.

Before concluding his argument, Chester knocked apart the four different defenses put forth by the defendant: alibi, accident, insanity and self-defense. Then there was one more, he said, namely character assassination of the prosecutor "in order to save his miserable hide from going to the electric chair, where he belongs."

Chester asked the jurors to deny the defendant mercy. "What are you going to give as your reason for mercy?" he asked. "When he cut her throat after she was down? When he jabbed her in the ear after she was down? When there are 17 different hammer marks on her head, inflicted after he cut her throat? Mercy! Mercy!

"Any way you want to figure it, he is guilty of murder in the first degree, and you cannot get out of it to save your life; you cannot get away from it," Chester said.

"Bring back a verdict that the whole state of Ohio is going to be proud of, a verdict that everybody knows is just and right!"

The courtroom erupted into applause – one reporter described it as "bedlam" – much to the consternation of an enraged Judge Scarlett, who repeatedly hammered for quiet and threatened the perpetrators with contempt of court. None was singled out, however.

"We were informed that at some time that there were certain parties coming out here to pack this courtroom to do that very thing," Seidel told the Court.

A courthouse regular who had spent many years as a defense attorney listening to prosecutors rip his clients described Chester's performance as "one of the most moving and telling arguments ever heard."

19 | DONE IN A DOZEN MINUTES

When the jury began deliberations at 3:57 p.m. Wednesday, August 14, six volumes bound in green cloth accompanied the panel to the colorless jury room serving Courtroom No. 1 The weighty books contained 2,749 pages of testimony by the defendant and 94 witnesses. The 11 men and one woman on the jury also had access to Theora's pistol – said to be the same model Leon Czolgosz used to assassinated President William McKinley in 1901 – a pocketknife, a hammer, various articles of bloodstained clothing and other items entered as exhibits during the trial.

Finally, they had Judge Scarlett's charge to them. The jurist spent 45 minutes detailing the applicable law. Seven verdicts were possible: first-degree murder, first-degree murder with mercy, second-degree murder, manslaughter, assault and battery, acquittal and not guilty by reason of insanity. Only first-degree murder carried a mandatory sentence of death in the electric chair.

Upon sitting down next to her husband at the defense table, Helen Snook adjusted her printed chiffon dress and the fashionable fur piece around her neck, then tightly grasped her husband's hand while Judge Scarlett read his charge. "Mrs. Snook Tries in Vain to Make Her Mood Fit Gay Frock" *The Ohio State Journal* reported. Snook's mother, dressed in gray and black, sat nearby, fanning herself and fighting back tears.

As the jury panel retired to deliberate, the two women joined Snook in his cramped jail cell. Extra guards stood by to prevent any incident, such as suicide. His mother's reassurances were again optimistic promises to her son: "The jury will probably take a long time. They will not be harsh to a college professor."

When all the jurors were in their room, nobody seemed to want to sit down and discuss the merits of the case. Groups of two and three gathered in the four corners of the room. Someone suggested that they first pray together. Charles S Baird, a slim, white-haired retired farmer from nearby Groveport and, at 70, the oldest member of the group, led them in what the portly Mrs. Cassady described as "a lovely prayer." They bowed their heads and asked for divine guidance.

Chosen as foreman, Baird called for an initial paper ballot. There was no need for a second one. After 16 minutes of prayer and 12 minutes "in deliberation," the panel had reached its verdict.[27]

"Every person on the jury tried to find some point in favor of Dr. Snook," said Juror Harold E. Brown, "but no other verdict was possible. I don't believe any man had a fairer jury."

So surprisingly speedy came the decision that it took more than 10 minutes to round up the principals in the case and get them back into the courtroom. Mrs. Snook and her mother-in-law returned across the Bridge of Sighs, through the sheriff's outer office and into the narrow hallway outside the courtroom. They chose not to enter to hear the verdict. Helen sat down on a top step of the landing; the older woman all but collapsed in a broken witness chair. Neither woman could hold back the tears. Attorney Max Siefert, standing by, felt helpless.

Suddenly, a door opened. It was reporter Karl B. Pauly of *The Ohio State Journal*, seeking a telephone. "Oops. Sorry," he said apologetically, upon spotting the weeping women. No sooner had he

---

[27] The 28-minute verdict was said to be the second-fastest in Franklin County's history. In December 1922, a jury took 10 minutes to find guilty Stanley Forbes, a notorious Cleveland gunman who killed a policeman.

secured the telephone than an uproar ensued in the courtroom. Another reporter poked his head out of the door. "It's first degree," he said to his associate and quickly left. In a muffled voice, Pauly flashed the news to his city editor: "Guilty. No mercy."

"I can't bear it! I can't bear it," the grieving wife sobbed, having heard the reporter's news. The loving mother did not immediately comprehend what was going on. "Tell me what it is," she implored Pauly, clutching his arm. She bit on her fan in grief. "Leave the door open so I can hear what they are saying about my Jimmy."

Pauly began to dictate his news to his city desk: "The cowardly story told by Dr. James H. Snook on the witness stand brought him no mercy..."

After Bailiff Carl Beck passed the folded paper to the judge for his review, it was handed to Court Clerk Joseph Palmer, who read the verdict to a breathless courtroom, electric with excitement. Near-pandemonium followed, as the gallery applauded and shouted its approval. Snook never flinched. He licked his lips, gripped the arms of his chair and stared straight ahead. Sheriff Paul and three deputies surrounded Snook. From where the former professor sat, he could hear his wife and mother sobbing. "Take them downstairs," he whispered to attorney Siefert. "I will see them there."

Once in a private room, the two women tried for a half-hour to console Snook, and he tried to console them. Reporters waited outside in an anteroom, dodging a bat – "a bird of evil omen," one newspaper said – that flew into their space. Then Sheriff Paul and his son, handcuffed to the felon, escorted Snook back to jail, and a deputy sheriff drove the two women home.

Dr. and Mrs. Melvin T. Hix, Theora's gray-haired parents, heard the verdict from the first row of the spectator section, where they had been seated earlier that day, out of the jury's sight. A few spectators cried softly upon watching the elderly couple enter the courtroom.

"It's Theora's vindication," the 64-year-old Dr. Hix said after the verdict. "[Snook] killed her, and he almost killed us. But we don't matter. Can you blame me for the way I feel about it?"

Ricketts, who promised appeals all the way to the United States Supreme Court, was not happy with the panel's decision. "That jury didn't deliberate anymore on its verdict than Dr. Snook did about this murder," he said. "It only goes to show that the jury, contrary to instructions, had made up its mind long before it ever went into the jury room, there to bring in a verdict not warranted by the facts and the law in the case." Judge Scarlett said he would hear a motion for a new trial the first of next week, then pronounced the sentence.

Mrs. Cassady was happy to get home with her husband and son. "I'm glad it's over. It is just like getting out of jail," she said. Facing her at home was her canning, two weeks overdue.

Out in the street more drama unfolded. The police raided a newsstand in the center of the city, at the corner of Broad and High streets, and confiscated several dozen copies of *The Murder of Theora Hix*, the abridged, unexpurgated transcript of the trial. Ed Manley, the owner of the stand, said he had sold about 400 copies at 35 cents each before the raid, although bootleggers advanced the price to $5.

New York journalist James L. Kilgallen wrote that "public approval of the verdict was expressed on all sides in Columbus today. Never has sentiment been so pronounced against a defendant here. Interviews with men in the street… could be epitomized in the phrase, ' Tickled to death that the jury gave him the limit.'"

In an editorial headlined, "Now the Air Seems Purer," *The Columbus Citizen* noted that it had avoided the publication of "unsavory details" from the trial. "No newspaper could print it… It was that kind of a story."

It certainly was that kind of story.

20 | NARY A THOUGHT

After the verdict, the people of Columbus were ready to carry Chester on their shoulders through the streets of the capital city. He had battled the forces of evil – namely, a smart-assed Ohio State professor – and won a decisive victory.

"TALK OF RUNNING CHESTER FOR CONGRESS SINCE THAT 28-MINUTE VERDICT CAME IN" shouted the headline in *The Ohio State Sunday Journal*. "The trial of the middle-aged professor is only the climax in a series of big cases in which Prosecutor Chester has defeated some of the adroit legal lights of the Ohio bar," wrote *The Journal*'s Davis W. Boman.

Others praised the "boy prosecutor" in other ways. Ray C. Womeldorf of the Federal Glass Company, presented Chester with a ball-peen hammer made of green glass that appeared remarkably similar to the murder weapon. It could be used to drive nails, the donor said.

"The highest commendation" was heaped on Judge Scarlett as well. "In a case so revolting in its very nature to every feeling of decency, almost any judge might feel tempted to err against the legal rights of the defendants in the interest of decency; but the clear insight of Judge Scarlett prevented any mistakes of that kind," *The Columbus Evening Dispatch* said in an editorial. "No judge could have managed a difficult situation better, and Franklin County may well be proud of such a jurist."

Dr. Hix and his wife thanked the judge for his "masterly handling of the case." They also expressed their appreciation to the prosecutor's office, the police, the reporters and the people of Columbus.

Snook gave no thanks. He relaxed in his jail cell, read magazines and newspapers, played a little solitaire and in the evening ate a hearty meal of pork and beans. Before dinner, a small group of reporters appeared, accompanied by Sheriff Paul and Deputy Sheriff Dale Thibaut. They observed a man totally at peace.

"Does the thought of paying the death penalty worry you, doctor?" a reporter asked.

"I never gave it a thought until you mentioned it," the poker-faced prisoner replied.

"Did you tell everything about this case when you were on the stand?"

"No," he answered. "I have lots left over. There are salient facts yet to be told."

"Is there any truth to the rumor that Mrs. Snook plans to divorce you?"

"No, indeed," Snook replied. "Run along now. I don't have anything more to say."

Later in the evening, Snook chatted with night jailer Tim Donovan. "Wasn't the trial an awful strain on you, doctor?" he asked.

"Oh, it wasn't any strain it all," the convicted man replied. "I never had any real interest in what was going on. The jury needn't even have gone into its room as far as I was concerned. With all the stuff [evidence] they had before them, I'm surprised that they went upstairs at all."

He had a restless night, however, and awoke with a headache.

Snook's attorneys pushed the appeals process forward, first with the motion for a new trial, arguments for which Judge Scarlett heard on Tuesday morning following the verdict. The defense took to task the jury for the speed of its decision, Chester's "brutal antics" and the incitement of the local citizenry against its client. However, convinced by the evidence that Theora's murder was premeditated, Judge Scarlett denied the motion and immediately launched into the sentencing.

"The defendant, James H. Snook, will now stand up," the judge ordered. Snook, appearing totally uninterested, did so, buttoning the bottom button of his suit jacket.

"Have you anything to say why the sentence of the Court should not be passed upon you?"

"No, sir, Your Honor." His eyes remained affixed on the judge.

"It is then the duty of the Court in accordance with the verdict of the jury and under the law in such cases impose the following sentence upon you: I sentence you to die upon the 29th day of November, by means of an electric current passed through your body of sufficient intensity to cause death, and passed through your body until you are dead."

Snook stood rock-steady, as if on the firing line.

For the fifth time in his judicial career, Judge Scarlett had pronounced the mandatory death sentence. Ricketts described it as "legalized murder. It is my belief that in time everyone will regret that this case has been rushed through."

Within 30 minutes, four deputies – Ralph Paul, Charles Norris, Bill Patrick and Bert Callahan – had Snook in a county car for the 13-block ride from the jail to the Ohio Penitentiary on Spring Street. A small crowd already had gathered outside the 95-year-old prison. Some were waiting for the daily tour of the penitentiary. Visitors paid 25 cents; children under 12 were admitted for free. Paul L. Weaver, who served as secretary of the Snook jury, was there, too, taking home movies of Snook's transfer.

It was a special day for Warden Preston E. Thomas, who greeted his new prisoner, one of nearly 4,500 in the miserably overcrowded 19th century penitentiary. This day he celebrated 25 years of service to the state of Ohio, 17 years as warden. In a few months he would face the worst prison fire in U.S. history, one that took 322 lives.

At 10:08 a.m. Snook, now No. 60656, entered Death Row in the prison's Annex, "... a place where death is forever lurking in greedy expectancy," wrote Marvin E. Fornshell in his 1907 history of the old Pen.[28] Before entering his cell, Snook underwent a strip-search by guards Earl Hostetter and Jeff Henderson. They found $4.45 in Snook's pants pocket. "You can spend it while you are here," Hostetter informed No. 60656.

Arthur Maul,[29] a cop-killer, and Joseph B. Locke, who killed his mother-in-law, greeted their new cellmate. "Hi, doc," Maul said, extending his hand. The cell contained two upper berths; Snook was assigned an upper. Next door, in cell No. 2, the Rev. M. Rhodes was quite impressed with the new death row arrival. "This is getting to be a high-class place," he commented. "There's a preacher and a doctor both here now." Prison officials recognized neither title, however.

The penitentiary served lunch shortly after Snook arrived. For his first meal, Snook dined on beef fricassee, whole wheat bread and ice water. The dinner menu included fried bacon and gravy, mashed potatoes, whole wheat bread and tea.

For a time Warden Thomas considered a daily bulletin covering Snook's menus, activities, health, etc. "This is not a matter of pandering to a murderer's public. It is a case of self-defense against a flood of inquiry we expect to receive from a sensation-loving world," the warden said. The bulletins were never issued, however, but Thomas made it known that he had in mind publishing a psychological treatise after the execution. He said Snook had "the coldest nerve of any man I know whoever sat in Death Row."

Although Helen visited almost daily – and sometimes twice a day – Snook complained of being lonely. "My present surroundings seem unreal to me, just like a bad dream," he said, describing prison as

---

[28] Marvin E. Fornshell, *The Historical and Illustrated Ohio Penitentiary* (Columbus, Ohio, self-published, 1907), 24.

[29] Maul was the only other one of the three incarcerated at the time to go to the chair. He was executed November 1, 1929.

"depressing." Subsequently, Warden Thomas and his secretary, Walter Kohberger, made a point of stopping by frequently to chat.

The appeals process began with the filing of a 35-page petition in error with the Second District Court of Appeals. On November 22, the judges of the appellate upheld the decision of the trial court. Three days later the defense filed a similar petition with the Ohio Supreme Court which led Chief Justice Carrington T. Marshall to issue a stay of execution until December 20.

On December 10, Helen Snook and Dr. Hix were among the largest crowd ever to hear arguments in the history of the Court. Arthur C. Fricke, a Cincinnati attorney hired by the defense, spoke for an hour, seeking a reversal of the first-degree murder conviction. He scored Chester for his assault on Snook to obtain a "useless" confession. Chester admitted the incident to the Court and said he had apologized. Assistant Prosecutor Gessaman also argued for the State.

When the court stayed the date of execution a second time – until January 31 – to allow more time for deliberation, it was widely assumed its ruling would not be forthcoming until the new year, but in a surprise move on Christmas Eve, the Court ruled against the defense.

Warden Thomas withheld the news from Snook until after the holiday. That evening cooks in the penitentiary's kitchens prepared 4,000 pounds of pork for Christmas dinner, along with oyster dressing, applesauce, candied sweet potatoes, blackberry pies, celery, bread and coffee. Cigarettes and cigars also were handed out.

The defense team, which now included Arthur M. Spiegel of Cincinnati in addition to Ricketts and Fricke, wasted no time in making their next move, an application for a rehearing before the Ohio Supreme Court. That petition was denied January 8, but two weeks later the Court stayed the execution a third time to allow time for petitions to the federal courts, including the United States Supreme Court. Snook's new date with death was February 28.

Ohio Governor Myers Y. Cooper sat on the sidelines, under no pressure to do otherwise. His office had received but a trickle of letters urging his intervention. In any event, he made it known that he would not consider any action in the case until all Ohio and federal options had been exercised by the defense. At the insistence of Helen Snook, Ricketts laid plans for a petition to the nation's highest court, asking it to review Ohio's most famous murder case.

Barely four days prior to the date of execution – specifically, at 4 p.m. Monday, February 24 – Ricketts and Spiegel presented their petition for a stay to Charles Evans Hughes, sitting for the very first time as chief justice of the nine-member U. S. Supreme Court. Chester waived Ohio's right to file a reply, thus clearing the way for the Court to immediately consider the brief. The proceeding ended two minutes after it began. A decision was expected the following day.

Ricketts immediately returned to Columbus to prepare for an appeal to the governor, sensing that would be necessary. Also returning to Columbus Monday night was Dr. Melvin Hix, who arrived from Florida and checked into the Southern Hotel. He said he intended to stay in town until after the execution.

Helen Snook cried in Warden Thomas' office when the news came from the Supreme Court. In a 18 words from Chief Justice Hughes, the Court denied a stay and review of the case. "The case of James Howard Snook against the state of Ohio: Application for a writ of certiorari[30] denied." Amid tears, she vowed to make one last frantic effort to save her husband.

She arrived at the Statehouse shortly before noon Thursday, heavily veiled in black. Her pastor, the Rev. Isaac E. Miller, held her arm to steady her walk. Realizing eager photographers likely would be awaiting her, another veiled woman – Helen's Junction City cousin, Mrs. Frank Landrum – went a few minutes ahead as a decoy, convincing most onlookers that they had seen the "almost widow." After the press dispersed, Helen slipped into the Statehouse and spent 31 minutes with Cooper in his private office. He expressed sympathy for her plea but gave her no hope.

---

[30] Judicial review.

Drained emotionally by the experience, Cooper sat quietly at his desk for a few minutes to gain his composure, while a dozen reporters waited outside. He wiped his eyes, then allowed the press to enter. His comments were brief and to the point.

"Mrs. Snook has just been here. It has been a very trying ordeal for me," he said. "I don't believe there is anything much to say beyond that." In response to questions, however, he explained that the woman had "told her story in a simple, straightforward fashion as finely as anyone could present it. She ... was composed throughout her recital," although she was under great strain.

"The law must take its course," Cooper said. "I have the deepest sympathy for Mrs. Snook."

In a last-ditch effort to get a review by the Ohio Clemency Board, Ricketts gained a 2 p.m. hearing with the governor. Also present were representatives from the Ohio attorney general's office, the Clemency Board and, once again, Dr. Melvin Hix, who appeared with his attorney. The governor announced that nothing presented to him would justify executive clemency, There would be no further stay: The execution would be held at the appointed time – 7:30 p.m. Friday.

Hix rushed forward and grasped Cooper's hand, saying, "Governor, I thank you from the bottom of my heart."

The gray and foreboding Ohio Penitentiary, trapping behind cold stone and hard steel a community of nearly 5,000 criminals, quietly waited for yet another execution. An ominous atmosphere prevailed. The hush at sunset was out of respect for a fellow felon who would soon pay the ultimate penalty with his life.

Snook did not appear ruffled at all. He smiled throughout a visit from his wife, mother, sister and brother-in-law. However, his 2-year-old daughter did not come to Death Row. He would never see her again.

Snook did not receive a lot of mail, but one communiqué came as a telegram from the Westminster Presbyterian congregation in Bradenton, Florida, where the Hix family worshipped. It asked that he make a clean and true confession of his sins and accept Jesus Christ as his Savior. They called his attention to 1 John 1:19: *God tells us, "If we confess our sin He is faithful and just to forgive us our sins and cleanse us from all unrighteousness."*

He also received a postcard that read, "All my love, from a former student." It bore a woman's signature.

Two pictures of Snook appeared in *The Columbus Dispatch*. One photograph had been taken in 1920, the year he won his Olympic medals, and the other in 1929. Readers could not help but notice his checkered necktie. He had worn the same tie through the decade. His conservative nature would not allow him to throw it out.

Helen stood fast beside her husband during his incarceration. "He has been a lesson to me every day," she said. Perhaps she saw him quite differently from the prosecutors and the press, who thought him calm, cold and calculating – a man accepting his destiny and, as the press put it, "who'd like to die sneering." Helen saw a different man, one who was doomed to pay the ultimate penalty with bravery and stoicism – locked in Death Row, facing it all behind the bars that confine him, but not complaining or whining.

Now the killer's fate was sealed.

21 | AT PEACE WITH GOD

Three women, all neighbors of the Snook family on W. 10th Avenue, "begged" Governor Cooper for permission to pull the three levers in the Death House, one of which would shock Dr. Snook into the afterlife.

The three were not alone. Nearly 500 others, mostly women, asked for permission to execute the former professor or to be present as a witness to his death, such was the outrage at the crime. A student at nearby Ohio Wesleyan University wanted to attend to improve his grades in his Science of Society class. A soldier at Fort Hayes, a post-Civil War military facility in Columbus, wanted to pull the switch to collect the $50 the State paid executioners. Paul D. Lucas of Indianapolis, Indiana, was one of dozens who sent a telegram to the warden. "Would it be possible," Lucas asked, "for me as a mortician to witness the execution?" All requests were denied; Ohio law did not allow women to be witnesses, anyway.

Prisoners and guards tidied up for the execution. They swept, mopped and scrubbed the Death House and installed a larger coal-burning stove in anticipation of the severe cold snap that forecasters said would move into Columbus late in the week. They also cleaned the bathtub on Death Row, where Snook would bathe shortly before taking his last walk.

A childhood friend from South Lebanon, Clifford Wesley "Tacks" Latimer, outfitted Snook with the blue shirt and pants he would wear to his death. It 1924, Latimer shot a police officer four times in the back and received life in the penitentiary. At the turn of the century, Latimer played five spotty seasons of Major League Baseball with five teams, hitting .221 in a career total of 27 games. Now he worked in the property room on Death Row.

"We never talked about his crime in here," Latimer said following Snook's execution. "We talked about sports, and things we used to do back home."

Latimer received a pardon for his heroic deeds that saved lives during the penitentiary's blaze which killed 322 on April 21, 1930.

Friday morning Helen awoke to read in *The Columbus Citizen* her husband's last interview, in which he likened his circumstance to "a shooting match. As you know," he said, "I was a champion marksman. When, in a contest, another man had a handicap on me, and I knew I was beaten, I didn't step out. I shot it out to the last and finished, a good sport. I am playing this game that way. ... I know how to control my nerves. I learned that shooting. One must face the bull's-eye with steady nerve. One learns to govern every muscle and every nerve. I learned that, too, in the operating room of the veterinary hospital. The hand must be steady when one cuts into the tender tissue; the eye must not falter. This training comes to me in good stead in this time."

To the last, Helen looked out for her husband. She asked the warden that he be allowed to wear his tuxedo for his last meal and she be allowed to join her husband for the final supper. Such requests never had been made before. The warden granted Helen her second request but denied her first.

She arrived at her husband's cell at 9:15 a.m. on the day of the execution, only to find him still asleep underneath a prison-gray blanket. It was a late awakening for a man who had told the jury he routinely rose at 7 a.m., but he had played cards with cellmates and then read magazines until 2 a.m. While the card game played on, there was cause for momentary alarm. During evening roll call in the guardroom, a guard accidentally dropped his pistol. It fired a bullet through the wall of the guardroom, missing everyone but injuring the guard's professional pride.

The Rev. Miller joined Helen while she waited in the caged enclosure outside his cell while her husband dressed. He downed a cup of coffee for breakfast – nothing else – and chatted with his wife, who stayed until 10:15. He picked at his lunch tray of pickled pork, hominy, dessert and coffee.

He lacked interest in his food and other routine matters, such as getting his last shave and haircut, a tonsorial process that usually began about 8:30 a.m. every Friday. This day, much to Snook's irritation, the barber was late. When he finally arrived and began the shave, Snook jocularly reminded him to be sure to use a straight razor on the top of his bald head to trim the 10 hairs residing there.

Moments of incertitude had passed earlier that day as he sat in his cell, pacing in his small confines. He did not see a song written by Julius Diehl that appeared in *The Ohio State Journal*. It was titled *The Death of Dr. Snook:*

Oh, James Howard Snook is my name,
Her dear name was Theora Kathleen Hix,
To the chair I must go for her murder,
And by dawn I'll be far o'er the Styx.
Chorus
From high to low estate,
Was my unhappy fate,
Like Lucifer I faltered, and I fell.

Helen returned to the penitentiary at 2 p.m. to accompany her husband on the short walk from his Death Row cell to the small, unobtrusive one-story Death House in the southeast corner of the massive prison. Flanked by three guards, the couple walked briskly, arm in arm, past cells occupied by the most violent, and out into the yard. The air was cool but the sun brilliant and almost welcoming for the condemned man, who had not been out in the fresh air since his incarceration in August - 192 days earlier.

Man and wife proceeded across O. Henry Field, the prison recreation area named in honor of author William Sidney Porter. As inmate No. 30668, Porter wrote *The Gift of the Magi* and other short stories while inside the Ohio Penitentiary.

After 300 yards or so, the couple reached the Death House door. Snook didn't hesitate. He quickly stepped inside and into the 9-by-15-foot, brightly illuminated, windowless, death holding cell. The whitest of white walls bore gruesome "official" photographs of those previously executed. For those seeing the pictures for the first time, it was a macabre scene. A chair, toilet, washbasin and wooden table on which the last meal would be served "decorated" the cell. Two space heaters helped cut the damp stored within the stone and brick walls. The three guards stood at the wooden second door, beyond which the electric chair waited for its 267 victim.

Snook's first cellmate, Arthur Maul, had sat in "Old Sparky" on November 1, 1929. He was No. 266.

Hours prior to the execution, the curious began congregating on Spring Street outside the 22-acre penal institution, the world's largest. By 7 p.m. more than a thousand cars and pedestrians all but blocked the street. It was a quiet, orderly crowd. Now and then someone asked a police officer, "Is he dead yet?" Despite the lateness of the hour, several individuals still sought admission in vain, including the Rev. Louis Cosillo, a Venezuelan journalist for *El Universal,* Caracas.

At the Governor's Mansion, 3 miles distant, a 24-hour police guard stood vigil, a routine security procedure when executions took over the night.

Snook took his last meal at 5 o'clock in the afternoon. It was a novel sight. Most doomed to die eat alone, but Snook dined with his wife; her first cousin, Mrs. Frank Landrum; the Rev. Miller; the Rev. Kleber E. Wall, the prison's Protestant chaplain; and Oscar Roedell, a grocer from

Pomeroy, Ohio, a close friend who had been Snook's roommate at Ohio State University.

Local newspapers described how "four colored men, dressed in white coats and caps," bore individual trays of chicken, mashed potatoes, gravy, creamed peas, Jell-O with whipped cream, ice cream and cake. The Rev. Miller followed with a large pot of coffee. As the plates were placed before the diners, no one spoke, but once the servers departed, all engaged in small talk as they ate what Mrs. Thomas, the warden's wife, had cooked. She was a trouper, having twisted an ankle earlier in the day.

"The meal was perfectly normal in every way," the Rev. Miller said. "No reference was made of the execution for the crime. Dr. Snook ate heartily." No one lit up a cigarette or cigar – provided by the State. (Snook did not smoke.)

Using white wine, the Rev. Miller administered Communion to the Snooks after the meal. Once finished, Snook spoke softly and privately to the cleric: "I didn't know how to appreciate my wife until now. Take good care of her. Don't forget, I repudiate that [the murder] was not premeditated." The statement was grammatically garbled, understandably so, given that death was but moments away.

"I have no fears in the future," he continued. "I do love my wife and all the things she has done for me. It took a bump to make me appreciate her, but it wouldn't have taken such a hard bump as this." And he added, "My peace is absolutely made with my God."

Snook had a couple of token "gifts" that he asked the Rev. Miller to distribute. One was his pince-nez which he gave to the cleric. The second was the maroon coat-sweater the professor wore in prison. That went to Luke W. Erwin, a fellow prisoner and former minister to whom Snook took a shine. Erwin, who was serving 20 years, regularly delivered meals to Death Row inmates.

The guard assigned to the last watch warned the assembled that time was up. As the guests departed, they left the Snooks in an embrace. He hugged her tightly and kissed her. Tears were in their eyes. He whispered in her ear, "Don't ever let the baby know."

"Never."

"Goodbye," he said.

"Goodbye."

For the last time they parted. She left the Death House, supported on each arm by the Rev. Miller and Roedell. She would wait in the warden's private quarters inside the prison while the minister returned to the Death House.

Historian and former Warden Marvin E. Fornshell described the night of an execution. "A deathlike stillness hovers over the whole prison as the executioners and attendants go with muffled tread to the Annex," he wrote. "On every hand you imagine that grim Angels of Death are lying in wait for their prey."[31]

Shortly before 7 p.m., 55 bareheaded men – primarily police officers, lawyers and journalists – were led into the Death House, two-by-two. Visible nearby sat a polished black hearse from the Schoedinger Co. mortuary, waiting for the dead.

"Show your tickets," a guard commanded. The witnesses, momentarily blinded by the brightness of the room, paused at the door – nervous, jittery – close to one another. "After you," said the first in line. A few whispers stirred the solemn scene. "Step in, gentlemen," another guard ordered, shattering the stillness.

Once in place and facing the stark reality of "Old Sparky" but a few feet away, the witnesses experienced "a feeling similar to your worst nightmare, multiplied a thousandfold," Fornshell wrote. "Entering the chamber of death you stand with bated breath, while your blood goes cursing through your system with an unnatural speed and your heart beats with the vigor of a smith's hammer on a Monday."[32]

It was 7 o'clock.

"Well," said Deputy Warden James C. Woodard. "I guess we're ready." He would stand in for Warden Thomas, who for several days had not been feeling well enough – it was food poisoning, he said – to

---

[31] Marvin E. Fornshell, *The Historical and Illustrated Ohio Penitentiary* (Columbus, Ohio, self-published, 1907), 24.

[32] Ibid.

perform his duty as executioner. Penitentiary physician Dr. George W. Keil stood by with his stethoscope projecting from his pocket. He and Woodard checked their watches.

Snook stepped into the room and blinked at its brightness. His last few steps were deliberate and without hesitation, but his eyes were red. Upon seeing the instrument of death for the first and last time, he didn't flinch. He immediately sat down in the wooden chair, pulled up his trouser legs as he did so and surveyed the room, as if taking classroom attendance. He leaned back on the headrest. As guards swiftly cinched straps to his wrists, waist, legs and under his chin, he appeared totally uninterested. He closed his eyes just before a leather mask slipped over them.

Snook said nothing, no final words.

In an adjacent room, three guards held three levers to be pulled in unison, but only one would send 1,950 volts to the chair. With a nod of his head, Woodard ordered the switches be thrown. The dynamos began to hum. A few witnesses turned their heads to avoid the sight of death. With surgeon's fingers, Snook clenched the arms of "Old Sparky."

"God be with you." Did Snook hear Rev. Miller's last words?

It was 7:04½ p.m. when the light above the electric chair flashed red.

Thump! Snook convulsively strained against the straps as the electricity delivered a stunning blow. His forehead turned crimson just above the mask. Red blisters formed on his pate. After 10 seconds, a pause, and then another jolt of 300 volts for 40 seconds. Dr. George W. Keil unbuttoned the top half of Snook's shirt, placed his stethoscope to the chest of the slumped figure and listened for a heartbeat. The doctor stepped back, listened again, stepped back and allowed two other attending physicians to listen yet again. Finally, at 7:09 p.m., Dr. Keil declared, "Gentlemen, sufficient current has passed through the body of James Howard Snook to cause death."

Helen Snook, who had borne her grief with grace, collapsed in the warden's quarters at the time of the electrocution, slightly injuring her ankle.

At 7:15 p.m. the Schoedinger hearse bearing Snook's body drove out the West Gate of the penitentiary, through the crowd on Spring Street and to the mortuary. There the body was embalmed, dressed in a black suit and black oxfords and delivered to the Snook home on 10th Avenue. Helen did not leave the penitentiary until almost 8:30 p.m.. By then the assembled had dispersed, convinced that the veiled "widow" they saw depart 30 minutes earlier in the company of Colonel Walter Collins of the Volunteers of America was Helen Snook. It was another deception.

Theora's father, who had been at a private dinner party, hurried to the elevator in the First National Bank building downtown and up to the offices of Boyd E. Haddox. Somewhat breathless, Dr. Hix arrived to be greeted by his Columbus attorney.

"It's all over," Haddox said, shaking his client's hand.

"It's all over? Thank God for that."

Dr. Hix plopped himself down in a chair to compose himself.

"What time was the execution?"

"7:09 p.m."

"Justice was in a greater hurry that I thought," Hix said with a smile. He telephoned the news to his wife, who had remained in Florida.

Unbeknownst even to the police, the funeral took place in the Snook home at 5 a.m., the Rev. Miller presiding. The short cortege then wound its way through downtown to the 360-acre Green Lawn Cemetery. The hearse, three limousines and a private car pulled up adjacent to the newly prepared Plot 243 in Section 87. It had been selected by Mrs. Snook several weeks earlier.

Eighteen mourners, bundled up against the misty, 26-degree cold, bowed their heads as the pastor read a prayer from the Bible. Under the dim light of dawn, the steel-gray casket was lowered into the ground, and it was over. No flowers and few tears, except for the widow's. In less than 30 minutes, the sexton's workers had the plot covered once more.

For decades, until 2005, the location of the professor's grave was kept secret at the family's request. In fact, the cemetery's record of

Helen Snook's lot (No. 68204) is clearly marked twice in capital letters: "DO NOT GIVE OUT LOCATION." The headstone is another deception. It reads simply, "James Howard 1879-1930."

Exhausted after the long, trying ordeal, the Rev. Miller could not mount the pulpit Sunday. An assistant, the Rev. Hugh S. Graham, conducted the morning service at the King Avenue Methodist Church

The death of Dr. Snook, Ohio State professor of veterinary medicine and Olympic champion, took place 260 days after the commission of the crime.

22 | A LOGICAL CONCLUSION

What was the true story behind Theora's murder? Was it premeditated or was it a moment of madness? Did a 24-year-old coed lust for the body of a man twice her age, demanding more and more of him until he could stand it no longer?

During his time in custody Snook told a number of tales to police, the prosecution, journalists, his attorneys, his family, the jury and the judge. Each time he twisted the story just a little and then denied what he had said. Just three days before the execution, Ricketts sat in the condemned man's cell and "pleaded with him to tell the truth."

Snook changed his story once again, at least on three points. First, his wife knew there was another woman because Theora would telephone the house, demanding to know the professor's whereabouts. Second, the "scar" on his penis was actually a birthmark, and third, the tale of "unnatural relations" was a fabrication, obliquely suggested to him by one of the physicians who examined him before the trial.

Perhaps Snook's last "confession," purportedly made during his final days on Earth, held the real story.

On the day of Snook's burial, Ohio Penitentiary Warden Preston E. Thomas made public the story he had held to himself as confidential or privileged information. It would be the most revealing of the things

Snook had not said earlier during the trial or before. As Snook had told his accusers: "You don't know the half if it. You are just guessing."

While incarcerated, Snook had time to think up yet another tale, one that he revealed only to Warden Thomas. Some accused the warden of making up the story, but according to him, over six months he frequently talked with his prisoner, promising to reveal nothing as long as the case was pending in the courts or before the governor. The execution of Snook in "Old Sparky" unsealed the warden's lips.

The final confession, as recalled by the warden, appeared in both *The* (Cleveland) *Plain Dealer* and *The Columbus Evening Dispatch*:

> Dr. Snook was naturally strong mentally and physically; his mind was well-trained, and he had attained a considerable degree of culture. He claimed to possess the power to direct his thought into any channel he chose, even to the extent that, while awaiting execution in the annex, he kept his mind from dwelling upon his tragic predicament except when conversing about it.
>
> I think his mentality was never questioned, but morally he was not even a moron. Some would say he was "unmoral," or that he had abandoned any sense of morals whatsoever: That is probably a gentler term - a distinction without a difference.
>
> This predominating trait in his character was selfishness. This trait was well-defined. It was the controlling factor and influence; he lived for self alone and for the gratification of his desires. He thought but little of the welfare of others and then only as it should be reflected upon himself. He had a tremendous ego and liked flattery when it was properly served up to him. His expression that he "admired intellectual people" indicated his attitude.
>
> His entire life was dominated by sex. I have often been asked if he was not conscience-stricken. That could not be, because he was almost devoid of conscience. There have been so many stories about this crime and the circumstances surrounding it that I have deemed it well that the truth be told.

At his trial, Dr. Snook testified in great detail regarding an alleged attack he said Miss Hix made on him. This testimony, Dr. Snook told me, was absolutely false in its entirety.

Snook's only regret [he said] was that "the story did me more harm than good and probably had something to do with the severity of the verdict."

He admitted to me that it was a grave mistake for him to have told this story because "it hurt his case."

During the first talk I had with him, he was at first reserved and dignified. This might seem strange in one under sentence of death, but in Snook it probably was an expression of a characteristic or habit, acquired in years of experience in the classroom, that had not then yielded to his new environment.

Soon, however, he grew very talkative, so much so that I had to tell him that I came to talk to him a little myself. I told him I did not want to talk to him at that time about his case and suggested to him that the time might soon come when, after due reflection, he might like to talk to someone frankly.

I told him just as frankly that I did not care to listen to a recital of the alleged facts as they had been supposedly revealed in his testimony, and I added that in my opinion the truth had not yet been told, that he knew this, and that nobody believed his story.

He took this kindly and then, to my surprise, he immediately admitted that the truth had not been told. He said he would want some time to think things over.

I gave him plenty of time to meditate, and some days later, when we talked again, he had lost his air of dignity; his head leaned forward, not upright, and he seemed very willing to talk what he termed "common sense."

In order to get properly started on the true story, the defense setup at the trial must be wiped clear out of the picture. Dr. Snook had pleaded self-defense. I pointed out to him that it was preposterous to advance the theory that a man of his strength would have to use a heavy machinist's hammer to keep a girl of that size and strength of Miss Hix from drawing a pistol from a handbag. I added, "Doctor, I would hate to think that a man of your mentality, and having the steady nerve you have proved you possess, would even have thought such a thing necessary."

He answered, "Well, you know that most of my defense was false."

This was the first admission I got from him, and it started him on the road to telling the whole truth. It was the crucial point. There was no way out except by a direct, straight route. The issue was not well-defined. It was in reality a yes or no proposition.

I said: "Doctor, there was then no reason for the statements you made on the witness stand, and no truth in them?"

His answer was: "No, except that it was a part of my defense."

He then went at length into the character of Miss Hix, as he saw it, and discussed her attitude toward him during the past year. He said that at times she would threaten to expose the whole affair and ruin him, socially and professionally.

He said her "tantrums" and fits of anger became more and more frequent and increasingly violent. With each one, he said, he had more and more difficulty in calming her; he never dared leave her until she was in good humor. Often she would telephone him at night when he was writing or working at his office, or would come there and rap on the window until he answered her summons.

This fear of disgrace and loss of position was a big factor, if not the biggest cause, that contributed to build up the attitude he had towards the girl at the time he made up his mind to kill her.

He told me also, that "things at the university were different this last year than ever before, as they were bearing down pretty hard," and that "a 10-cent defalcation [embezzlement] now was important as a $10,000 theft a year ago." The constant worry and nervous strain was another factor that contributed to the attitude, which made it possible for him to commit the murder.

He then said that the two of them used exciting or stimulating drugs, but not, as he had testified, for experimental purposes. He told me that he deemed the use of drugs for himself more or less necessary because of his age. Then, as the stimulating effect wore off, there was a corresponding and inevitable period of mental and physical depression, and during these periods, he said, he felt nothing but disgust for Miss Hix and the whole affair.

"I don't know that I like the word *disgust*," he continued. "You tell me the word. I prefer a word not quite so strong." He admitted that the feelings of disgust, or repulsion – the desire to repulse the girl – registered continuously stronger and deeper until these feelings grew almost unbearable.

He told of the time when Miss Hix had prevented him, by her objections, from visiting his mother and said that at that time, "my feeling against her was very high." This helped lead up to the final scene.

On the Sunday afternoon before he killed the girl, Snook was in the midst of a golf game when she telephoned him. A little later, she came to the clubhouse in a taxicab and went out on the course and insisted that he accompany her back to their room in town. This incident happened during one of his periods of depression, and it was then that he made up his mind to kill the girl. As he told me, "Something had to be done to stop the whole affair."

From that time on, he planned how to carry out this decision. "The instruments of death – the hammer and knife," Snook said, "I always carried with me."

He made the final decision to carry out his plan to kill the girl when ... they met on the night of the murder [and she said] she "did not want to go to the room that night but preferred to drive out into the country." The opportunity had occurred; he drove to the rifle range and carried out his decision.

He drew a queer distinction. While admitting "premeditation," he said that the murder was not "coldblooded," but that events of the past year had been such as to cause him to be in such a frame of mind that he doubted his ability to have acted otherwise than he did. To him, the killing was the logical and inevitable conclusion.

He admitted that the mutilation of the body was planned to make the crime appear the work of a fiend. This came when I reminded him about his first statement was that "I could not have done it – it was the crime of a degenerate."

His employment of a private detective to run down the trail of a mythical "fiend," who, he said, had twice threatened Miss Hix, was a natural outgrowth of his plan for the killing.

It will be recalled that after the murder, he drove back to town, bought a paper, went home and cooked a lunch.

"Doctor," I asked him, "why were you not all wrought-up and nervous after the killing?"

"It was such a relief to have it over," he answered and then he added, "You know one grows nervous over sudden impulses." He added that he was "surprised" when he was even suspected of the crime.

Thus, just as the nation's Roaring '20s came to an end, so did the life of Dr. James Howard Snook, veterinarian, Olympic champion, and murderer. On the immediate horizon loomed the stock market crash of 1929 on Wall Street and the advent of the nation's worst depression.

✱ EPILOGUE

Immediately following her husband's execution, **Helen Snook** reverted to her maiden name, **Marple**, which she also gave to her daughter, **Mary**. They lived a fairly quiet existence in the same home on 10th Avenue. Helen resisted university circles in an effort to save herself from hearing painful gossip among university women's groups. Even in changing her name, her anonymity wasn't complete. For a time, she taught at Linden Elementary School in Columbus, then moved into the Olentangy Village retirement home. She died October 11, 1978, at the age of 88.

Mary Marple grew up in Columbus and attended Ninth Avenue Elementary and University School, a local high school. A classmate remembered that Mary "was a marvelous girl and dear friend. She was strikingly beautiful as she grew – blond, tall and slender, and she moved with incredible grace. In school, her friends didn't know who her father was. She never mentioned him, and I never saw a picture of him in their home. I guess I didn't really think much about whatever happened to her dad. My mother knew that one of the girls in my class was the 'Snook girl,' but it took me awhile before I realized that it was my good friend."

After graduating from high school, **Mary Marple** attended Wellesley College, married, had a son and taught at the prestigious Punahou School in Honolulu, the same school President Barack Obama attended.

Snook's mother, **Mrs. Mary Snook,** died June 13, 1933, in Lebanon, Ohio. His father, **Albert,** died March 15, 1927.

Helen's parents, **James D. Marple** and his wife, **Carrie,** watched over their daughter and granddaughter. They lived adjacent to Helen, in the same 10th Avenue double.

John J. "Jack" Chester, a Republican, ran for the county prosecutor's office again but was defeated. He never held public office again but prospered in private practice. Biased political factors circulated out from the Democratic camp that said he had pushed the Snook trial through too fast. They also questioned his tough, strong-handed tactics.

Chester died July 15, 1957, following surgery at the Cleveland Clinic. He was 58.

Assistant Prosecutor Myron B. Gessaman became a member of the Ohio House of Representatives (1934-35) and mayor of the city of Columbus (1936-39). He died in Mt. Carmel Hospital August 20, 1975.

Defense attorney Ernest O. Ricketts died April 22, 1941, following a heart attack. He was 71.

Defense attorney John Franklin Seidel passed away February 8, 1965.

Chief of Detectives Wilson G. Shellenbarger suffered a bowel obstruction and died April 28, 1950, at the age of 78.

Chief of Police Harry A. French died April 3, 1975.

Theora Hix was buried June 20, 1929, in a family plot at the Floral Park Cemetery, Johnson City, New York.

Melvin Hix and his wife returned to Bradenton, Florida. When they left Columbus, Dr. Hix said: "Thank God! Now our minds are at rest. Justice has been done." He died in 1944; she died three years earlier.

The Snook home at 349 West 10th Avenue was torn down some years ago to make way for an enlarging of the University Hospital complex.

The "love nest" rooming house at 24 Hubbard Avenue gave way some years ago to redevelopment in the area now called the Short North.

The Ohio Penitentiary, the world's largest when it was built, was torn down in 1998. The redeveloped area is now called the Arena District.

The New York Central Railroad rifle range is today a Columbus Police Department firing range and multi-use facility.

Snook's Ford Coupe – "The death car," as some called it, was put up for sale by Ricketts and Seidel. It was like new except for the fact that the seat was shredded by investigators seeking evidence of blood. A police officer offered $350 for the car. Chester stopped the sale, saying that the proceeds should go toward paying court costs. Eventually, the car was sold and is now in the hands of a collector in Columbus.

Dr. David White's letter to **President George Rightmire** in the Ohio State University archives reflects the defense and the feelings of a man who has been asked to resign his position as dean after 34 years. It mentions that in his years as a teacher and administrator, he served four different university presidents, and that he had been able to deal with discipline cases under each with a different procedure in each case. There were many discipline cases solved within the department that White touched upon and dismissals with the approval of the former presidents. There were many references to his acts in dealing with problems of the veterinary college regarding disciplinary action of several faculty members. White writes:

> The Dean is always liable to damage suits should he make, through error or misunderstanding, a false report against an apparently delinquent member of his faculty. In the Snook case, in so far as I am involved, I feel I, in no way, evaded any responsibility. I think

the evidence shows that I proceeded <u>at that time</u> much as any prudent, cautious dean would have done in dealing with a delinquent who for many years had carried the title of full professor in a great university. Under the academic cloak, he carried on affairs so secretly and skillfully that not even his most intimate associates discovered them. No one in the department knew anything of his greater moral delinquencies. As with the President so with the Dean in matters of this sort, they are the last ones to learn about them. The great fear of 'becoming involved' promotes secrecy. Since the tragedy I have been told so many stories about Doctor Snook, valuable pieces of testimony which I most needed in presenting my case, but, except as stated in this document, I knew of nothing about beyond what seemed to be rumor and very little of that. It must be admitted that an affair of this kind would not ordinarily result in murder. It seemed prudent at that time to take no action until the investigation was complete. The question is, therefore, what would a prudent Dean have done in this case which I did not do?

Respectfully submitted, David S. White, Dean

White sent a formal one-sentence letter to President George Rightmire on September 5, 1929 – between the end of the trial and execution of James Snook. It stated simply, "After completing thirty-four years of teaching and administrative work at Ohio State University, I herewith resign as Dean of the College of Veterinary Medicine."

But a more personal and a sadder note followed:

"My dear President Rightmire: As you did not call me night before last, I assumed something else interfered. Your letter announcing change of the date of the board meeting from Monday, September 9th to Saturday, September 6th did not reach me until about noon today. I called your office by phone at 12:10 but got no response. I enclosed the resignation as I promised before the investigation began, and in response to your suggestion that if I did you would recommend for me a teaching position."

At the following meeting of the board in late September, the minutes state, "that the resignation of Dr. White as Dean of the College of Veterinary Medicine be accepted and that his services with the university be discontinued as of this date." His resignation was accepted without comment.

It was believed that White had withheld information from police about Snook. He had not fired Snook, whose immoral lifestyle was becoming more obvious. It also seemed by most that White had allowed drugs to be too available. Having to appear under subpoena in court for the defense was no help to his relationship to the department. According to those who remember him, he'd worked most of his life to build up the college; he didn't want to say anything to help destroy it.

It was obvious to White family members that factions in the university forced his retirement to absolve themselves from the embarrassing status of the veterinary department. White was blamed for not having acted to oust Snook and, after the fact, it was obvious he should have.

White remained friends with President Rightmire and particularly with Oscar Brumley, who became dean when White left. White and his wife, Mabel, became somewhat reclusive and dropped away from university groups, maintaining a summer home in Estes Park, Colorado, and playing cards with a few friends occasionally. He died of a heart attack in his sleep in 1944. He is buried next to his first wife, Nellie, in Green Lawn Cemetery. Snook is buried there, also.

Mabel White never was accepted by the University Women's Club, particularly because she had been White's secretary during his first marriage, and she was only a year older than White's daughter, Lana.

In 1920, four years before the death of White's first wife, Nellie, the dedication page of his book *Principles and Practice of Veterinary Medicine* is to Mabel, who had helped with the proof reading and indexing. His marrying Mabel a year after Nellie's death was seen in some university circles as an insult to Nellie's memory. She had been active in a number of women's groups and was held in high esteem. She and her husband were known for their fine dinner parties among faculty members.

Mabel White was delighted when she was told where her crypt would be. It is in a wall of the little domed chapel at Green Lawn Cemetery. Her place of rest is next to former Ohio Governor James A. Rhodes and his wife. Mabel died in 1991.

A family note: Dean White was the grandfather of Nancy Pennell, whose name is on this book.

✻ AFTERWORD – THURBER'S TALE

The story of how *The Columbus Evening Dispatch* obtained its big scoop on Dr. Snook's confession was told by humorist James Thurber in his book *The Thurber Album: A Collection of Pieces About People* (Simon and Schuster 1952 New York pp. 231-233).

"Norman Kuehner," Thurber began, "got the biggest exclusive news story of his career one day in 1929. He had the title of assistant managing editor then, but he was still a police reporter at heart. Five days earlier, the body of an Ohio State coed named Theora Hix had been found on a rifle range five miles north of the city, and Kuehner had followed every line of the murder story in all three Columbus papers. A lot of evidence pointed at James H. Snook, professor of veterinary medicine at the university. The county prosecutor had been unable to break the suspect down, but every time Kuehner's phone rang, he was sure he was going to hear the news that Snook had confessed. He hoped to hell the story would break for the afternoon papers.

"It was a little past noon, on Kuehner's fateful day, when *The Dispatch* man at the police station phoned him and said, 'Shelley just told me he's going to eat lunch at the usual place today. Made quite a point of it.' Shelley was Wilson G. Shellenbarger, an old friend of

Kuehner's who had been a patrolman when young Gus[33] covered the cop house, and was now chief of detectives. The 'usual place' was a restaurant at Spring and High streets where Kuehner sometimes had lunch with Shellenbarger. He was excited, but he kept his voice low and casual as he said into the phone, 'OK, I'll wander over there,' and hung up. He stuck some folded copy paper in his pocket and hurried to the restaurant.

"When Shellenbarger showed up, he told Kuehner that Snook had confessed a few hours earlier but that the story was going to be held for the morning papers. He explained that William C. Howells, Columbus representative of *The* (Cleveland) *Plain Dealer*, had been allowed to visit Snook in his cell that morning, together with another newspaperman. Snook had repeated his confession to them, and Howells had agreed to take the stand at the trial, and corroborate the state's evidence, if the prosecutor would hold the story for the morning papers. Shellenbarger wanted to give his old friend Kuehner a break, and he did. He poured out all the facts in the case, including the details of the long and gaudy affair between a college girl and a professor that led up to the murder. Half an hour later, Kuehner hurried back to his office with a dozen pages of notes and began to hammer out his story. He was about half-finished when the county prosecutor's office phoned to announce that a conference of newspaperman would be held there at three o'clock that afternoon. Smallsreed[34] was sent to represent *The Dispatch*, and told to stick close to the prosecutor until four o'clock. When he got back, at five-minutes after four, with an official carbon of Snook's confession, he was handed a copy of *The Dispatch's* late afternoon edition, which had just hit the street. Kuehner's long and vivid story, interspersed with photographs, covered the whole front page.

"Kuehner's big story was unsigned, and there was no mention of Shellenbarger's part in it. It wasn't until two years later that Smallsreed

---

[33] A nickname for Kuehner.
[34] George A. Smallsreed

found out who wrote the story and where it came from. Kuehner didn't get any glory at the time but he had the deep satisfaction of knowing that he had scooped the world on one of the biggest murder stories of the century. The ex-police reporter of *The Columbus Dispatch* had had his greatest hour."

Thurber was a reporter for *The Dispatch* a few years before the Hix murder.

✳ BIBLIOGRAPHY

The arrests, trial and execution of Dr. James Howard Snook made headlines in virtually every daily newspaper in the United States. Following are the names of the reporters and the publications whose work was most rewarding in the research for this book.

Newspapers

The Cincinnati Enquirer: Wilmar G. Mason.
The Cincinnati Post: Alfred Segal.
The Cleveland News: Dan W. Gallagher.
The (Cleveland) *Plain Dealer*: W. C. Howells, J. C. Daschbach, Gordon Barrick.
The Cleveland Press. Earl Minderman.
The *Columbus Citizen*: James C. Fusco, Harry F. Busey, Frank R. Ford, Pauline Smith, Harry Keys, Belford P. Atkinson, F. M. Heller, James T. Keenan.
The Columbus Evening Dispatch: Arthur C. Johson Jr., George A. Smallsreed, Charles C. Williams, Anne Schattenstein, Marion Fosnaugh, Kenneth D. Tooill, Milton Caniff, George Tucker, Hugh Fullerton.

The New York Daily News: Irene Corbally Kuhn, Joe Costa.
The New York Journal/International News Service: James L. Kilgallen.
The Ohio State Journal: Karl B. Pauly, Mary V. Daugherty, Howard R. Thompson, Harry J. Westerman, Clyde D. Moore, John C. McConaughy, Fred Allhoff.
The Ohio State University Lantern: Emmett M. O'Connor.
The Toledo Blade: William H. Mylander, Dixie Tighe.

News Services, Syndicates

Associated Press: L. R. Penn, K. E. Hopping, Perry D. Wellser.
International News Service: James L. Kilgallen, John A. Artz .
United Press: Morris DeHaven Tracy, Leslie D. Harrop, Garland Hick.

Books

H.M. Fogle, *The Palace of Death* (Columbus, Ohio: H.M. Fogle, 1908).
Marvin E. Fornshell, *The Historical and Illustrated Ohio Penitentiary* (Columbus, Ohio: Marvin E. Fornshell, 1908).

✳ INDEX

.41 caliber Remington derringer, 35, 38, 96, 99, 106, 110, 112

A

appeals, 151, 153, 156
   for a new trial, denied, 156
   to Second District Court of Appeals, 156
   to Ohio Supreme Court, 156
   to Governor Myers Y. Cooper, 156-158
   to Ohio Clemency Board, 158
Art of Love, The, 30, 96

B

Baird, Charles S.,
   jury foreman, 65
   leads jurors in prayer, 149
Berry, Dr. John H., 49
Boulay, Louis A., 99
Bowen, Freda, 26, 73
Bracken, Raymond (Ray) C., 2, 3, 7, 89

Brown, Ralph O., 35, 137
Brumley, Dr. Oscar P., 28, 75, 88, 89
Bustin, Alice, 12, 13, 69
Bustin, Beatrice, 11

C

Caniff, Milton, 52, 184
Cassady, Mrs. Harry (Betty), 65
Chester Jr., John J., 10, 25, 131, 139, 176
   slaps Snook, 79, 133, 137, 138, 140
   final argument, 144
   cross-examines Snook, 87
   interrogates Snook, 138
Cloud, Emmett, 9
Cooper, Governor Myers Y., 156

D

defense rests, 136
Dillon, Bertha, 14, 70
Druggan, Charles Sumner, 99

INDEX 187

drugs, xii, 30, 59, 61, 69, 73, 98, 172
    Spanish fly, 68
    marijuana, 76, 98
Duncan, Judge Robert P., 45, 46

E-F

Edwards, Peggy, 13
fellatio, 104
final words, 143, 166
    at execution, 166
    for the defense, 143
Franklin County Grand Jury, xiii, 28, 43
French, Columbus Police Chief Harry E., 176
Fricke, Arthur C., 156
Fusco, James C., 79, 184

G

Gaver, Dr. Earl E., 45
Gessaman, Myron B., 35, 58, 139, 176
Glenn L. Myers Mortuary, 10, 12
Guy, Deputy Sheriff John W., 9, 10

H

Hamilton, Bertha Snook (sister), 3
Heffner, Dr. G. W., 49
Harrah, Dr. Frank W., 132
Hicks, Paul C., 58, 139
Hix, Dr. Melvin, 46, 131, 157, 158, 176
Hix, Theora K., 11, 16, 17, 35, 72, 131, 176
    birth, 18

education, Northfield Seminary for Young Ladies, 16, 18
    Ohio State University, The, 19
    arrested with Meyers, 16
    breaks off relationship with Meyers, 97
Howells, William C., 52, 79, 184
Hunter-Trader-Trapper, 6
Hyde, Dr. Arthur C., 54

J

Johnson, Ephraim, 71
jury deliberates, 149
jury foreman, 43

K

Keil, Dr. George W., 166
Kilgallen, James L., 51, 94, 136, 151, 185
Krumlauf, Paul "Krummy"
    finds murder victim, 71, 81

L

Landrum, Mrs. Frank (Lilly), 93, 157, 163
last meal, 161, 163, 164
    menu, 161
    six in attendance, 163, 164
Latimer, Clifford Wesley "Tacks"
    boyhood friend to Snook, 161
    prison inmate, 161
    former major league baseball player, 161

Lavely, Howard, 10, 30, 43, 84, 144
Lindbergh, Charles, 50
Long, Charles F., 76
love letters to Theora, 30
"Love nest", 26, 27, 32, 37, 65, 74, 98, 100, 103, 108, 118, 132, 177

M

marijuana, 76, 98
"Mabel", 111, 114
Marple, Carrie, 176
Marple, James D., 176
Marple, Mary Snook (daughter), 175, 176
May, Corporal John B., 9, 71
McCall, Detective Robert, 10, 27, 37, 53, 108, 109
McPherson, William, dean of the graduate school, 13
Meyers, Marion T., 21, 85
    arrested as suspect, 21
Miller, The Reverend Isaac E., 28, 39, 157
Miller, Milton
    finds murder victim, 8
Murder of Theora Hix, The, xi, xiii, 120, 151
murder weapons
    ball-peen hammer, 23, 76, 84, 152
    pocketknife, 23, 35, 38, 42, 43, 84, 107, 127, 137, 140, 145, 146, 148
Murphy, Dr. Joseph A.
    testimony at trial, 71-73, 139, 142
    autopsy details, 9-11, 22, 32
Murray, Clarence R., 53, 70

N

New York Central Railroad rifle range, 8, 27, 53, 65, 177
Nichols, Earl, 13

O

Ohio National Guard, 5
Ohio Penitentiary (Columbus), 177
    Death Row, 155, 158, 159, 161, 162, 164
    last meal, 161, 163, 164
    Helen Snook's visits, 155
    electric chair, "Old Sparky", 163, 165, 166, 170
    Arthur Maul, cellmate, 155, 163
    Joseph B. Locke, cellmate, 155
Olympic Games, xi, 3, 89, 93
oppressive heat, 120

P

Palmer, Joseph H., 94
Paul, Deputy Sheriff Ralph, 41
Phillips, Detective Otto Warren, 10, 26, 27
pocketknife, 23, 35, 38, 42, 43, 84, 107, 127, 137, 140, 145, 146, 148
press coverage of trial, xi
Pritchard, Dr. William C., 45

R

Ricketts, Ernest O., 24, 176
Rightmire, Ohio State University President Dr. George W., 28, 177, 178

INDEX 189

Roedell, Oscar, 163

S

Scarlett, Judge Henry L., 48,
   appoints psychiatrist, 54
   charges jury, 148
   sentences Snook, 154
Scarpitti, Romeo "Romy", 99
Schanfarber, Edwin J., 31, 32, 90, 91, 95
Shellenbarger, Columbus Chief of Detectives Wilson G. "Shelley", 10, 23, 27, 28, 35, 39, 81, 91, 108, 109, 176, 181, 182
Scioto Country Club, 24, 27, 51, 65, 76, 99, 119
   Theora ruins golf game, 100
Seidel, John F., 24, 139
Seyfert, Max C., 48, 139
shooting skills, 2, 3
Smalley, Margaret M., 25
Snook, Albert L. (father), 3, 4, 45, 176
Snook, Helen Marple, 1, 2, 15, 23, 28, 30, 31, 34, 45, 61, 62, 76, 90, 93, 95, 107, 118, 144, 146, 148, 149, 155-157, 159, 161
   at trial, 118
   at home, 175
   appeals to Governor Myers Y. Cooper, 156, 157
Snook, Mary Keever (mother), 3, 61, 176
   death, 176
   hears verdict, 164
   testifies, 106
   visits jail, 75

   visits Ohio Penitentiary, 172
Snook, James Howard, 2, 157, 162, 166, 174, 178
   at arraignment, 43, 45, 46
   arrested, 58, 62, 73
   boyhood in South Lebanon, Ohio, 3
   burial at Green Lawn Cemetery, 169
   confessions, to police, to journalists, to warden, 34, 35, 38, 39, 41, 50, 55, 79, 80, 110, 130, 133, 137
   dismissed from Ohio State, 28
   divorce talk, 32, 51, 62, 81, 91, 153
   education, at The Ohio State University, xii, 1, 5
   funeral service at Snook home, 167
   headstone a deception, 168
   horoscope, 64
   "love nest" (see "love nest")
   married to Helen, 2
   at Ohio Penitentiary, 154, 158, 163
   professor, at The Ohio State University, xi, 1, 2, 5
   salary, 118
   slapped
      by Theora, 98
      by Chester, 79, 133, 137, 138, 140
   at sentencing, 154
Spanish fly, 68, 75, 76, 132
spectators jam courthouse, 45, 52, 53, 157
Spiegel, Arthur M., 156

INDEX

T

Tarbell, Robert C., 45
Thomas, Preston E., warden, 154
    reveals Snook's final confession, 169
Thurber, James 34, 181, 183

U-V

United States Supreme Court, xii, 151, 156
    Chief Justice Charles Evans Hughes, 157
vasectomy, 113, 123, 133
verdict, 53, 54, 139, 147, 149-154, 171
Van Skaik, Detective Larry, 10, 11, 22, 23, 74, 108

vasectomy, 112, 113, 123, 133
Vorbau, Dr. W. H., 54

W

Wall, The Reverend Kleber E., 163
Weir, Bailiff Mayme, 100
Western Reserve University, 112
Westminster Presbyterian, Congregation, Bradenton, FL, 158, 159
White, David S., dean of the College of Veterinary Medicine, 87, 177, 178
White, Mabel, 179, 180
Williams, Dr. Guy H., 54
Woodard, James C., 165

✳ ABOUT THE AUTHORS

DIANA BRITT FRANKLIN is the author or co-author of a dozen books, including her most recent, *The Good-bye Door*, a multi-award winner in true crime and featured on television's *Investigation Discovery* channel.

Born in England but raised in the United States, she began her career with *The New York Herald Tribune*. Subsequently, she held various editorial posts – from reporter and columnist to section editor and managing editor – at two other daily newspapers, *The San Antonio* (Texas) *Light* and *The Columbus* (Ohio) *Dispatch.*

She also served as press relations director for Lincoln Center for the Performing Arts; and as director of public relations for Avis Rent A Car Inc. She presently heads Franklin & Son, a corporate pr consulting firm in Columbus.

For more than 25 years, Franklin also wrote a syndicated cooking column for Universal Press Syndicate. She resides in Dublin, Ohio.

ABOUT THE AUTHORS

NANCY SANOR PENNELL attended Ohio State University, majoring in fine and commercial arts. She was the director of The Heritage Museum, Columbus, for a number of years. Her grandfather, Dr. David S. White, was dean of the Ohio State University College of Veterinary Medicine at the time of the Theora Hix murder. Having heard of the story most of her life, she teamed up with Diana Britt Franklin for the writing of *Gold Medal Killer*. Mrs. Pennell lives in Dublin, Ohio.